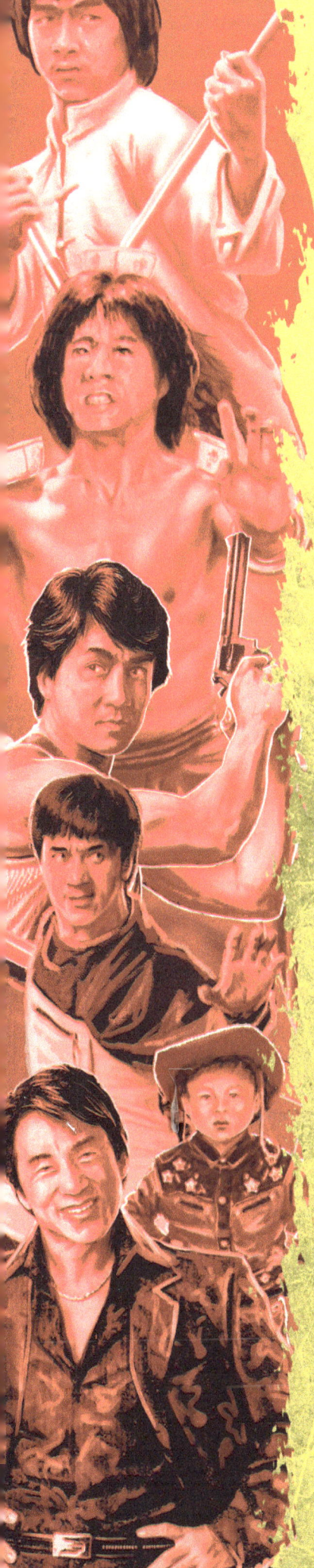

JACKIE CHAN SPECIAL 70TH BIRTHDAY EDITION

EDITORIAL

Welcome to a spectacular celebration of one of cinema's greatest icons! In this special edition, we're raising the curtain to honour none other than the legendary Jackie Chan on his 70th Birthday. Join us as we embark on a journey from the daring stunts of a fearless stuntman to the international superstardom of a beloved cinematic hero.

Prepare to be captivated as we delve into the heart of Jackie Chan's illustrious career with exclusive insights and interviews. Get ready for an in-depth conversation with the acclaimed director Brett Ratner, the visionary behind the iconic Rush Hour Trilogy, offering a unique perspective on the man behind the action. But that's not all! We've opened the floor to fans from every corner of the globe, allowing them to share their boundless passion and unwavering admiration for Jackie Chan.

In addition to our stellar line-up, we're thrilled to present a treasure trove of articles penned by esteemed writers such as Fank Djeng, Thorsten Boose, Mike Nesbitt, and Simon Pritchard. Their unique perspectives and profound insights illuminate the extraordinary journey of a true cinematic legend.

This issue is more than just a tribute; it's a heartfelt expression of gratitude from fans that have stood by Jackie Chan through thick and thin. So, join us as we raise our glasses and toast to the man who has inspired millions with his unparalleled courage, humour, and sheer cinematic brilliance. Happy Birthday, Jackie Chan – here's to a lifetime of thrilling adventures and unforgettable moments!

Rick Baker

CONTENTS

- 4. Introduction
- 8. Brett Ratner Interview
- 20. Action & Power (with Thghorsten boose)
- 26. Hands of Stone
- 32. The Wonder of Shanghai Noon
- 36. Jackie Chan Fanclubs
- 68. FanZone
- 94. An Ode To Wheels on Meals
- 96. Frank Djeng Talks Jackie Chan
- 103. 5 Fingers Of Discs
- 110. The Stuntman who became a Legend
- 114. The Dynamic Duo
- 116. Memorabilia with Emilio Alpanseque
- 120. Poster Gallery

CONTRIBUTORS

Emilio Alpanseque / Thorsten Boose / Johnny Burnett / Frank Djeng / Mike Nesbitt / Carl Trail / David Ghallagher / Gareth Smith / Harriet Connor / Hing HL / Jamie MacDonald / Phillip Gillion

JACKIE CHAN

A Living Legend & Timeless Inspiration

INTRODUCTION

In the fast-paced world of show business, where stars often shine brightly only to fade away just as quickly, there exists a rare luminary whose brilliance has endured the test of time. As the sun rises on yet another April day, we stand in collective admiration to celebrate the unparalleled legacy of Jackie Chan. For over seven decades, this titan of cinema has dazzled audiences worldwide with his boundless energy, unmatched skill, and infectious charm, leaving an indelible mark on the hearts of generations. Jackie Chan: A Guiding Light of Perseverance and Passion for more than six decades, Jackie Chan has transcended the role of a mere entertainer, becoming a symbol of perseverance and a testament to the power of passion. From his earliest days in the spotlight to his current status as an international icon, Jackie has consistently exemplified dedication to his craft. His journey from a young martial artist in Hong Kong to a global superstar is a testament to his unwavering commitment to excellence.

Martial Arts Mastery and Dazzling Choreography One of Jackie Chan's most enduring legacies is his mastery of martial arts and his innovative approach

to choreography. Throughout his career, he has pushed the boundaries of action cinema, choreographing breathtaking fight scenes that blend intricate martial arts techniques with elements of physical comedy. From the iconic ladder fight in "Police Story" to the gravity-defying stunts in "Drunken Master," Jackie's action sequences have set a standard for excellence that few have been able to match. Heartfelt Performances and Cultural Impact Beyond his physical prowess, Jackie Chan is also celebrated for the depth and authenticity of his performances. Whether portraying a lovable goofball or a hardened martial arts master, Jackie brings a level of emotional depth to his roles that resonate with audiences on a profound level. His ability to transcend cultural boundaries and connect with viewers from all walks of life is a testament to his universal appeal and enduring impact on popular culture.

The Humble Hero:
Jackie Chan's Enduring Humility Despite his status as a global superstar, Jackie Chan remains remarkably humble and grounded. Throughout his career, he has maintained a down-to-earth demeanour and a genuine appreciation for his fans. His humility serves as a reminder that true greatness is not measured by fame or fortune,

but by the impact one has on others and the legacy they leave behind.

A Beacon of Inspiration and Youthfulness
As Jackie Chan enters his eighth decade, his boundless energy and youthful spirit continue to defy the passage of time. He serves as a beacon of inspiration for aspiring artists and dreamers around the world, reminding us all that age is just a number and that passion knows no bounds. Whether performing gravity-defying stunts, or lending his voice to important social causes, Jackie Chan remains a tireless advocate for positivity and perseverance.

Conclusion: Celebrating Jackie Chan's Timeless Legacy
As we reflect on seven decades of Jackie Chan's spectacular career, we are reminded of the profound impact he has had on the world of cinema and beyond. From his ground-breaking action sequences to his heartfelt performances, Jackie Chan's legacy will continue to inspire and entertain audiences for generations to come. So here's to Jackie Chan, a true master of his craft, a beacon of inspiration, and a living legend whose light will continue to shine brightly for years to come. Happy birthday, Jackie – may your days be filled with as much joy and wonder as you have given to the world.

BRETT RATNER
JACKIE CHAN'S LEGACY: BRETT RATNER'S PERSPECTIVE

BY RICK BAKER (TRANSCRIBED BY KAREN CAMPBELL)

Rick Baker - So Brett, let's go back to the beginning and look at your awareness of Jackie when you were younger and the inspiration that led to 'Rush Hour'.

Brett Ratner - When I was a kid I can remember, well actually I can't remember what the first one was!

RB - I think you have said it was a video when you were 8 or 9, could of been 'Drunken Master' or 'Snake in Eagle Shadow' one of those early period ones.

BR - Yeah, that was what I was going to say, when I was 8 or 9 years old, I grew up in Miami, I don't remember if it was cinematics or, I know I saw it in the theatre, but I continued watching all of Jackie's early films and of course, Bruce Lee with 'Enter the Dragon' and 'Fist of Fury', but it was always Jackie for me, for a kid who, you remember me telling before, I was practicing martial arts , I was studying martial arts...

RB - Was this before you were introduced to Jackie? or had heard of Jackie? Or was seeing Jackie an inspiration to start learning martial arts?

BR - No, before, I think I was like 6, I started studying 'Japanese Okinawan Karate', I think I'd seen 'Enter the Dragon' but I discovered

Jackie in '*Snake in Eagle Shadow*' and of course '*Half a Loaf of Kung Fu*' and '*Drunken Master*'. I mean I was devoted, I was watching 'Spiritual Kung Fu', 'The *Fearless Hyena*', every movie that had come out I tried to see and then in 1981, I was about 11, I saw '*Cannonball Run*' and I thought 'oh my god', Jackie is in a Hollywood movie, it was such a shock to me, you know to see him, because he was such a cult figure for me, he was specifically 'Hong Kong' and I was such a big fan, and when I saw him, I thought he was under utilised. It wasn't until I was around 13 when I saw '*Project A*' and I was like 'holy shit!!', I'd forgotten that he'd done '*Cannonball Run 2*' which I was surprised because he had such a bad experience but it was around that time that '*Wheels on Meals* came about', then I remembered '*The Protector*', right, that was his other American movie?

RB – Yeah, he did 3 attempts at America, he did '*Cannonball Run 1*' and '*Cannonball Run 2*' and then James Glickenhaus did '*The Protector*' which obviously he went and reshot because he didn't think it was that great.

BR - Yeah, so the movies were to be my early homework, and as he was attempting to do the US versions, the Hollywood movies, I noticed that they were sub park compared to, for instance '*Police Story*'. Already in 1985, a year before going to NY (New York) film school, I'd already done over a hundred tournaments. I quit martial arts around the age of 13 after many years of competing. I loved martial arts. I loved Jackie's movies, I think one of my favourites was '*Project A part 2*', and' then of course '*Police Story*' and '*Police Story part 2*' and these movies just blew my mind.

RB - What captivated you, was it seeing Jackie performing martial arts, doing 'Buster Keaton' style stunts or his on screen character charisma?

BR - It was his charisma, character and his persona, not just his physicality because no-one can do physically what Jackie can do, but it was his dynamism, his charisma on the screen, he was a true movie star. He gave so much to the audiences watching his work, he was committed to satisfying them, and he was born to do what he did. Then in around 1992 when he did '*Supercop*' that was the beginning when I thought 'oh wow', Jackie's trying to stay true to his Hong Kong roots. I could tell that he wanted to do something bigger, then in 1995 '*Rumble in the Bronx*' comes and the title alone is what triggered me. At the time Miramax or maybe Newline, released '*Drunken Master 2*' and the other studio released '*Supercop 2*', and then, '*Crime Story*' would then be released by the other studio, back and forth, '*City Hunter*' '*Supercop*' alternating releases of Jackie Chan movies. It was then when I saw '*Rumble in the Bronx*' that I thought 'holy shit', I realised there's a movie, a pure Hollywood movie that was inspired by the Hong Kong cinema that Jackie did. There was an opportunity that I thought I could put him in a buddy cop action comedy because that was the genre, and, if I combine him with Chris Tucker that I worked with on '*Money Talks*', and take what he attempting to do in '*Rumble in the Bronx*' which he didn't quite achieve, he Americanised it, Hollywoodised it, as best he could, but still wasn't what it could be, but he mastered the genre. He himself was trying

to breakout and expand it for a worldwide audience, and I know Jackie, what he really wanted was to be a star in the United States because if you made a hit movie in the States it would travel the world. The Hong Kong movies were cult right!, and then I remember he did '*First Strike*', then I think it was around the time he made '*Mr. Nice Guy*' and then he went on to film 'Who am I ', oh and he did a cameo in an 'Alan Smithee' film: '*Burn Hollywood Burn*'. I'm sure they tried to put him other movies that he passed on. He was itching to fit in somewhere, but this was a Jackie Chan special, my idea '*Rush Hour*', a film written for Jackie Chan, created for Jackie Chan, starring Jackie Chan to try and stay true to his Hong Kong roots and his core fan base. He never wanted to alienate them, but I know he was more excited to make a hit in the United States so basically, I flew to South Africa and met with him for lunch. I gave him the key elements, I didn't know how he was going to respond, he listened and he didn't really say anything but I think he heard me. I said "Jackie, you've been making movies longer than I've been alive", I was 27 years old in 1998, a kid still and I said to him "We have to take your 20 minute fight sequence and turn it into 2 minutes, we've got to take the villain and really build a character because with all due respect, the villains in all your films are all stuntmen, faceless bad guys. Remember 'Rumble in the Bronx' the big fight in the grocery store, the audience has to hate a villain as much as they love you". Again, he didn't respond but I think he heard me because I was very specific. I said "Chris Tucker's verbal comedy and your physical comedy are going to be an explosion in a bottle". The only thing I didn't know for sure was if they had chemistry and it wasn't until they met and they spoke for 40 minutes and Chris Tucker said "I love you Jackie Chan", he kept saying it over and over again. We walked out of the room and Chris said "we have a problem" I said "what's the problem?", Chris said "Jackie Chan don't speak English, can we make a movie with Jackie Chan?" I said "yes, it's going to be great". When I go into the room I said "Jackie, do you like Chris?" Jackie said "I like Chris but I don't understand what he says". I said "This is going to be genius".....

This is what I mean by chemistry, I had nothing to do with it, the combination between these two guys was the explosion in the bottle. Jackie Chan never stopped doing what he did, he loved his Hong Kong fan base, and they probably weren't that impressed with 'Rush Hour' because the action wasn't as spectacular as what he does in his other movies. I had a set schedule and a set budget, I had parameters, safety issues, so many things, I'm not making excuses, the focus was on the characters and the relationship between the characters, and not necessarily the action, yes we had big stunts, big action sequences and then, Jackie did 'Shanghai Noon' with Owen Wilson which is one of the producers of 'Rush Hour'. I liked the movie but I don't think Owen and Jackie had the chemistry that Chris and Jackie had, I think the movie isn't as memorable as 'Rush Hour', of course I'm biased , I don't want to knock it, I think Jackie was excellent in it, but the problem with it which is the antithesis of what I did is why you remember Jackie in that movie which is the mistake the studio/director/producer made going back to 'Cannonball Run' was that they treated Jackie like a foreigner, like a bumbling foreigner, 'Shanghai noon' did that as well, because he spoke broken English, they wrote him as that character, whereas I wrote him as a foreigner visiting LA from Hong Kong, Jackie Chan is cool. I put him in a cool suit, I gave him a cool haircut, a modern haircut, he didn't want to cut his hair, and he said he'd rather wear a wig because every time he had his hair cut, he would have an accident. What was that movie when he fell from a tree?

RB – That would be '*Armour of God*' Brett

BR - '*Armour of God*', right. So he was very suspect of cutting his hair and he believed in superstition and stuff so he didn't want it cut. I convinced him, I said "trust me", and I made him cool. His strength came from being silent in the beginning of the movie, letting

全米No.1超ヒット!!
はやくも興収1億ドル突破!
（約140億円）

コイツらをハリウッドは待っていた!!

全米9月公開オープニング歴代No.1!

クリス・タッカー×ジャッキー・チェン
ラッシュアワー
ブレット・ラトナー監督作品

監督:"27歳の新鋭"ブレット・ラトナー/原作:ロス・ラマンナ/脚本:ジム・コーフ,ロス・ラマンナ/製作:ロジャー・バーンバウム,アーサー・サルキシアン,ジョナサン・グリックマン
製作総指揮:ジェイ・スターン,レオン・ドゥデヴォア/撮影:アダム・グリーンバーグ/美術:ロブ・ウィルソン・キング/音楽:ラロ・シフリン
1998年/アメリカ映画/ニューライン・シネマ製作/カラー作品/スコープサイズ/ドルビーデジタル,SDDS,DTS/サウンドトラック:マーキュリー・ミュージック エンタテインメント/ギャガ・ヒューマックス共同配給

Chris talk a lot of 'shit', and then he showed him that he does speak English right and in between Jackie did 'Tuxedo', 'Accidental Spy', he did 'Shanghai Knights', 'Shanghai Noon', 'The Medallion', 'Around the World in 80 Days', again, another example of Jackie being a foreigner in a way that he is an outsider and he's typecast. 'Rush Hour' always made Jackie cool, he's a guy who will educate Chris on how to take a gun away, Chris shows Jackie how to dance, they both have their fish out of water kind of elements. But, 'Rush Hour' is what it is because of Jackie's persona of how I see him, I see Jackie on the highest pedestal there is, I see Jackie like a 'God', like the coolest guy in the world, not because of his knowledge, his accomplishments or his career but by what his abilities are, I see him in that way. 'Rush Hour', is Jackie Chan through my eyes, and that's why it's relatable and adaptable and why it was so commercial successful. I put him on the highest pedestal and I think he really appreciates that and recognises that and that's why ultimately he loved the 'Rush Hour' movies. You know, his English is not always good so whenever he makes a comment about it or knocks it, it is because he has humility and he's like "I didn't know if it was going to be funny until I sat in the audience for the Premier" and I was "oh my god", people were laughing and clapping and cheering" and he appreciates a good big commercial movie. Can he compete on the action?, no, you know, he can't, not even close to the stunts he pulled off in those early movies.

RB - Do you think it was at the end when he watched 'Rush Hour' that he saw your vision? or do you think he gathered what you was trying to achieve as the filming went on?

BR - He connected all the dots and that's why we made two other movies because he saw what I was trying to go for, he thought "why is Brett going for so many takes of dialogue, spend the time on the action, focus on the stunts, make the stunts better, make the action better". The humour was always driven by the character, when he said "what's up my N****r", it motivated a fight, it didn't just become a fight because the black guy's in the room and a Chinese guy walks into their domain, he antagonised it, he created that hysterical line, racist of course but it's hysterical because it comes from the situation and not from a line from a joke. The humour comes from the situation, the situation that these characters were put into and that's where Jackie couldn't follow it, he didn't understand why Brett is

spending so much time on this character development, why is Brett spending so much time on dialogue, on lines, the nuances and the timing, because comedy works better in a master or a wide shot, you don't cut to the joke in a close up. He thought it was easy to clean it up, he didn't get it, just go in tight, but you can't cut to the joke, it's cheap so I had to work with timing, it's about a rhythm so Jackie and Chris's banter, you watch their banter. Remember when he says "you don't like to talk because you don't talk in that bla bla bla", that was a winner, them, going back and forth and if I could of manipulated that with editing, it wouldn't have been as good. So yes, it wasn't until Jackie saw the first 'Rush Hour' that he knew and once he got it, he understood, that is when he really rose to the occasion and that is why 'Rush Hour 2' is better than 'Rush Hour 1'. 'Rush Hour 1' was like he was blind and I was leading him and he had a leap of faith in me, he trusted me, he was like "okay I'm all yours, tell me what to do, he was frustrated because of the safety issues, we had to protect his safety and I wanted to make sure nothing happened to him because he was always doing dangerous stunts and wanted to do them without the wire, without protection, he had his team right there around him, he felt invincible but by the time we did 'Rush Hour 2' he got it, he understood the tone.

RB- I loved part 2, casting John Lone as the villain is what makes that film for me, he plays such a good baddie.

BR - Yes, and again, this comes from me being a fan. Everything in 'Rush Hour' is my fandom of loving John Lone from 'The Last Emperor', from 'Year of the Dragon' with Mickey Rourke. All these characters that I brought into the story, I knew that I had to surround Jackie and Chris with great actors, once you surround them with great actors, they rose to the occasion. Jackie is, believe it or not, isn't just an action star, and that's why he got an honoury Oscar because in his movies he gives so much heart, there are so many poignant moments that he could pull off the dramatic moments in his films because of his ability to make those moments believable and no-one doubts his abilities to pull off those dramatic moments. You believe him when he thought he found Chris Tucker dead in the movie, he was sad, he was listening to that Puff daddy song the tribute to Biggie, but my point is Jackie is one of those rare comedians, more so like the silent era stars like Buster Keaton, Charlie Chaplin, Harold Lloyd who he admired the most, who could pull off the dramatic moments the most, they had to do it without words, they had to do it with emotion, and, so for me, working with Jackie was one of the greatest experiences of my life and I learned more from the three movies that I did with him than I did in my entire career because he has a different way of making movies, it's the practical way, to me he is a film god, I told you before , this guy knows my job, the grip's job, the gaffe's job, the AC's job, the cinematographer's job, he can edit the film, he can literally do anything on a film set including sweeping the floors.

RB - Did he find that frustrating wanting to be part of everything rather than just being the star?

BR - Look, him knowing everyone's jobs seems to raise everyone's game; everyone works their arse off on Jackie Chan movies, not just my movies. They want to please him, he will just grab the camera, edit it himself, light it, do the stunt, direct it, he will do anything, so when he trusts you it's because he respects you. I was very proud of the respect that Jackie gave me. I wasn't intimidated by the fact he had directed dozens of movies and starred in hundreds, he had an incredible generosity of spirit of his knowledge and experience and after 'Rush Hour' he went on to do more Hong Kong movies, some animations but then he comes and does 'The Foreigner' which is a perfect example of a film which is really well done with great director Martin Campbell and he accepted that Jackie is an older guy so he plays someone older but he was so good in a dramatic role. I know Jackie can do anything, comedy, drama, action, he can do a musical, I would love to do a musical with Jackie, which would be unbelievable. 'Rush Hour 4' the musical (laughs).

RB - I mean, Jackie is in the latter part of his film career, yet he continues to work a lot , we see him still with a full slate of film that he has agreed to make.

BR - Hardest working person I've ever met.

RB -Do you think it would it be better to see Jackie behind the camera and look for new protégé, I see Jackie right now still beig able to be very physical in front of the camera, I would love to see him return to the old school films he would make a great 'Sam Seed' with a new protégé in a 'Drunken Master' reboot.

BR - I think when he is in his 70's, 80's he will probably become one of the great action directors, I mean, he is already one of the greatest action directors. You are right, he should take on a young protégé, train him, teach him, direct him, shoot him and he could probably direct a movie that's as good as uh 'Police Story', he could do it himself. He can design the action, design the stunts, choreograph everything, direct and shoot it, he can do anything. I was contemplating after 'Rush Hour' to go and live in Hong Kong and live up under him and be on his set because the guy is just a phenomenon. He really is, there is no-one like him. Like I said, he compares to Buster Keaton, Charlie Chaplin, Harold Lloyd, these guys too made 100's of movies. Now a director can make 1 movie a year maybe 2 years, some directors work every 5 years, Quentin Tarantino works every 6-7 years. I was trying to look to see how many films he's actually done, as credited as an actor.

RB - I believe it to be well over 100 films now.

BR - It's incredible, and Jackie will never stop, his whole life is creating films, creating cinema, entertaining people, he was born to do what he does.

RB - I think his testimony is that he is still at the top of his game, there's no real new people coming in, it's the same faces for many years, Sammo Hung, Andy Lau, there's not been any new big Hong Kong actions stars of their note, and Jackie has maintained that level, his age has slowed him down but he can still deliver on screen.

BR - Jackie is the ultimate; I don't think that there'll be another Jackie Chan, with the decades of cinema that he's created as a film maker. It's clever what they are doing with '*Karate Kid*' making him 'The Master' and that's an acting thing, but what I'm saying is, Jackie as a stunt coordinator, choreographer, action director, film director, in one fell swoop could he make one of the great action movies of all time?, probably, as a film maker, there are directors working into their 90's.

RB - I never knew why he didn't go back and make '*Drunken Master*' a reboot with him as 'Sam Seed' now he's that age along with a protégé, I don't know why no-one has pitched that idea to him.

BR -That's a good idea.

RB - I spoke with Jackie and asked him what his favourite film was and he said "really my favourite film is *Snake & Crane Arts*

of Shaolin' in that film, I did everything I could do to try and impress the director". If you look at that film, I am at my peak so I showcased everything I could to impress the director. This is my Favourite film."

BR - I loved the film where he played Sammo's brother, what's that one called?

RB - Well, that's another great one, you've got 2 titles, 'Heart of the Dragon' or in some countries it is known as 'First Mission'.

BR - I love 'Heart of the Dragon'. You were just saying what a good idea it would be having Jackie playing the old Master in 'Drunken Master'?

RB- The best thing that Jackie could do in my humble opinion , the whole of his worldwide fan base would love to see this, if you went to most people and asked what their favourite Jackie film is, would be 'Drunken Master 2' or 'Drunken Master' and I was talking one day to a group of people and they were saying that now Jackie is getting to that age where he is 70, he can play the Sam Seed guy lounging in the hammock drinking not doing too much, if they need to double him, they can give the stunt guy the grey wig and make a very easy double and here is where he can discover a new person who can take over the legacy, and he becomes the next one.

BR - Who could play his part?

RB - I do not Know, this is what I said, you could go looking for the next 'Jackie Chan', there is someone out there not been discovered yet, make a great film with a great back story discovering the new Jackie Chan.

BR - Jackie has more than just physical talent, Jackie is a movie star, and there are very few huge movie stars.

RB - Yes, There is someone out there with the 'X factor', they are just waiting to be discovered.

BR - It's like Michael Jackson, it's like people can dance like Michael Jackson, can imitate Michael Jackson but Michael Jackson had a persona that was like no-one else.

RB - Yeah, you can't be an impersonator; you've got to be your own person. I remember years ago they offered me big money, Charles Heung who owns 'Wins Films' and his wife, very rich, they were friends of mine. He wanted me to scour the world for the next big star for his film company and it all fell through, the stock market crashed, he said go the China go to wherever you need to go to find him and we can develop him. Even now, I see Sammo Heung looking for new protégés, you can't just be a fighter, you have to be everything, and have star quality that people want to watch. There are many Kung Fu films out there; there are good fighters and people like to watch.

BR - Again, nobody compares to Jackie. But I like this idea of another 'Drunken Master' I'll mention it to Jackie and see what he says, it's such a classic.

RB - That's the one to get behind, that's the film that I've said for a long time, he doesn't have to do everything, you can put a stuntman in there quite easily because they've got that little hat on with the head padded with a straw like wig.

BR - Let me watch it again, the only thing that I think about remakes like 'Police Story' was always a great idea for a film but it was flawed, all those Police stories are sequels. A true remake should be made with films that are flawed but have great ideas. 'Drunken Master' is not just a great film, a great idea, it's really well done, I mean it's a classic. It would be hard to see someone else playing Jackie's part but there will probably be some forgiveness. First of all, this would be a good

idea because young kids today don't know 'Drunken Master' although they know Jackie Chan. That's one thing on the plus side why the movie should be made, and if he is in it as the 'old guy' it sort of give it his approval. There'll be hard core fans that'll be "are you crazy, you can't redo that movie, it's a masterpiece".

RB - Yeah, but if Jackie is in it, it could be remade in Hong Kong, and then there is the one where Jackie and Sammo parted company, Jackie went on to do 'Project A Two' and Sammo made 'Eastern Condors' and now you imagine doing that now, making "Eastern Condors" like the 'Expendables' with some of the old actors like Sammo Heung, Yun Biao, they become this veteran group that go in with nothing to lose, they've never done a Chinese Expendables, if you watch 'Eastern Condors' which is my favourite film and inspired the name of my company 'Eastern Heroes', its flawed, but a fantastic movie. It's was a bit like 'The Deer Hunter' meets a Hong Kong war film, but that's the film where you can cast the older generation that has still got these fans for these older generation actors, like the Japanese guy Yasuki Kurata in 'Fist of Legend' and of course Jet Li, you could bring them all in. So Sammo took his group of people and went with Yuen Woo-Ping to make his film, Jackie got his stunt group and went head to head with his movie. It was 'Project A Two' v's 'Eastern Condors'.

BR - Do you think 'Eastern Condors' can be remade?

RB -"Absolutely, envision it akin to 'The Expendables': gritty yet poignant, boasting a cast comprised of the individuals previously mentioned. It would be exceptional. They even did a live stage show showcasing one of the fight scenes.

BR - They did it live?

RB - Yeah, they did a ten minutes live action sequence; some of them were from 'Seven Little Fortunes' so still flexible to showcase their acrobatic skills.

BR - Wow!

RB - They are the films to look remaking, bring Sammo back on, it was his 'baby'.

BR - I love Sammo, I love Sammo so much so, to sum up Jackie. I think Jackie's generosity of spirit and passion for movies and the fact that he was born to do what he does is what has made audiences around the world such a fan of his. What they don't really know about him, is that working with him is like what I imagine it would have been like to work with the old masters of the silent movie world like, Charlie Chaplin, Buster Keaton and Harold Lloyd. If I told Jackie I have a

50mm lens he knows exactly how many feet away to stand away from the camera. If i tell Jackie which way the light is coming from, he knows which direction to turn, whereas a lot of actors you have to walk them through and show them where their marks are, how to hit the light, the focus. Jackie knows if he is an inch too close to the lens on a specific long lens, he knows if he's an inch too far back. He is the master of cinema. He really is one of the film gods because he just understands every aspect of making a movie, he knows how to do every single persons job and beyond that, he knows how to entertain audiences. His generosity of spirit is what makes him 'special', because he wants everyone, not only the other actors, he wants them to shine, he is there for the assists. He is not about hogging the screen; he wants the actor next to him to be just as great.

RB - Can I just jump in there, I met with Hwang In Sik, the guy who Jackie fights in '*Young Master*', he said " I love Bruce Lee but I was killed in ten seconds, but Jackie, he let me beat him first time so I could shine".

BR - That's what makes him special; he wants everyone to shine, from the other actors, to the director to the crew. He wants them to feel good about their work at the end of the day, to feel that they have been a part of something that they contributed to and added to the value and the quality of the movie. Every film I make is 'my baby'. Jackie understands the importance of this, there's not a moment of wasted time, he's constantly thinking, dreaming, sleeping. As he's eating, as he's working he is thinking how do I make this better, how do i make the director happy, how do I make my actors happy. He'll come back from lunch and say " I have an idea", he's showing me this whole thing to help Chris (Tucker), he knows that Chris is handicapped when it comes to martial arts, he's not a martial artist, he's just a normal guy so Jackie is always trying to design, create things that'll make Chris shine and look as good as Jackie. There is no actor like him, most actors are narcissists, selfish, self-absorbed, wanting the camera to be on them, saying lines slow so they have more screen time. Jackie is a giver and people feel that and sense that. More than anything, his generosity for me was like I was on a Jackie Chan movie even though it was my movie, like taking a Math test with a calculator. He use to come up with ideas and say try this, this came about through his experience. He recognised that I knew what looked good in martial arts too and through this came about mutual respect. Greatest experience of my life and something that I am very proud of and I know Jackie is proud of it too. It was 26 years ago, I was only 27.

RB – Well, I want to thank you Brett for taking time out of your busy Schedule to contribute to this Special Jackie Chan issue celebrating his 70th birthday and keeping the world entertained.

BR – My Pleasure Rick, glad to be a part of this.

BRETT RATNER   RICK BAKER   KAREN CAMPBELL

ACTION & POWER

Training with the Jackie Chan Stunt Team in Beijing, 2024!

By Thorsten Boose

Who among us hasn't wanted to spend a day in the gym or on the set of an action film with Jackie Chan and his stunt team? A bit of sparring to warm up, then a few choreographed fights and the art of falling, Hong Kong style, to warm down. And how cool would it be to be a permanent member of the team? You're still allowed to dream.

Only a few have been able to fulfil this dream and actually get the opportunity to work with Big Brother and the Sing Ga Ban in films. The demands are extremely high. But now even beginners – whether as martial artists, stunt performers or action filmmakers – can put their skills to the test, learn and network with the original stunt team at Jackie Chan's Beijing training centre. I've summarised everything you need to know here. So, take your chance to be discovered and apply for the JCST Action and Youth Camps in the Year of the Dragon, 2024!

Philip Sahagun, American Shaolin
For decades, and that's not even an exaggeration, Jackie Chan has been inspiring his own fans to turn to martial arts or filmmaking. Fans became stunt performers, stunt performers became actors, actors became filmmakers. And one motto of the Jackie Chan family is that people support each other with experience and respect. A fan from the USA, holder of the 4th Degree Black Belt in Kenpo Karate and 34th Generation Disciple of Shaolin Temple, Philip Sahagun, has managed to open the doors of the JCST training centre to the world public. Philip Sahagun is a martial arts champion in both forms and fighting. With a background in American Kenpo, Kickboxing, Wushu and Shaolin Temple Kung Fu, Philip is a 7-time National and a 3-time international level martial arts champion. Philip has been a semi-finalist on "America's Got Talent", as well

Philip Sahagun

as a contestant on two of China's top-rated reality competitions, "Kung Fu Star" and Jackie Chan's "The Disciple". In 2008 and 2009, he toured as a martial art 'Ninja' performer for Tina Turner's 50th Anniversary World Tour.

He has taught martial arts extensively and represented America twice at the World Traditional Wushu Festival in China where he won both gold and silver medals for the U.S. Team. More recently, Philip Sahagun, joined world renowned performing arts company Cirque Du Soleil, performing three years as a solo artist before becoming a coach and choreographer for the company. To date, seven of his students have been offered contracts to perform in Cirque Du Soleil, five of which signed on to become full-time artists. In 2020, Philip Sahagun, together with his wife Ulziibayar, became the proud owners of K-STAR Training Academy and continues

to lead international workshops and seminars on the martial arts. When Jackie Chan announced in April of 2007 over his birthday that he was beginning a new reality TV show entitled "The Disciple", the aim of the program was to find a new star, skilled in acting and martial arts, to become Chan's "successor" and student in filmmaking. After sorting through a number of candidates from throughout the world, Philip Sahagun along with his U.S. team mates arrived in Beijing October 2007 to begin filming and face eliminations. As the only "Caucasian" allowed into the competition, Philip faced many challenges, including memorizing and acting in a foreign language, but it was a welcome learning experience. After four rounds of intense evaluations Philip received a special award for standout performance and made it to the top 20 before facing elimination. The finalist received training by Jackie Chan Stunt Team members Alan Ng and He Jun and competed in various fields, including explosion scenes, high-altitude wire-suspension, gunplay, car stunts, diving, obstacles courses etc. It was years before Philip had the idea of setting up his own training programme for martial arts and film enthusiasts with the Jackie Chan stunt team in Beijing. The time had finally come in 2023 with his now established K-STAR Training Academy. This is how initiator Philip Sahagun summarises the 1st JCST Action Film Camp:

"This summer I had the honor of creating / coordinating the first ever International Training Camp with the Jackie Chan Stunt Team. It was an amazing journey filled with incredible moments and incredible people. I would like to express my thanks and appreciation to the JC Stunt Team Director He Jun for trusting me with this task and wanted to give a shout out to all the staff and participants who brought this landmark event to life including Maile @mereaccumulation Kyle @thatkyleshapiro Jerry @kungfujerry the JC Stunt Team and the entire JC Office

Team working behind the scenes. You all did such stellar work and I look forward to developing new events next year!" (source: www.kstarcamps.com)

The 1st JCST Action Film Camp, 2023 Location: Beijing | Date Camp 1: 14 August 2023 – 24 August 2023 | Date Camp 2: 28 August 2023 – 07 September 2023

This is your once in a lifetime chance to train with Cinema Icons the Jackie Chan Stunt Team in Beijing.

The first event seemed to appear out of nowhere in the summer of 2023. But until then, a lot of sweat had gone into the planning. Thanks to social media and an event trailer, 41 participants, 35 men, 6 women, were able to apply for the prototype of a new exciting stage in the Jackie Chan stunt team's existence. The content shared on Instagram, YouTube, TikTok etc. during the summer and afterwards still bears witness to an event that fans of Jackie Chan have been dreaming of all their lives. A unifying cohesion between nations and cultures confirms Chan's simple philosophy of life: Love & Peace. This sporting experience was crowned with a joint song, as befits a Jackie Chan project. Without further ado, all participants were formed into the newly founded "Group Singalong" (a very clever play on words with Jackie Chan's Cantonese and Mandarin name Sing Lung/Cheng Long) and found themselves in the recording studio, where they recorded "Sincere Hero" (真心英雄) together as a team anthem. On the Instagram channel of the Jackie

Chan Stunt Camp it was written: "As part of our experience we were tasked as a group to sing one of Jackie Chan's songs '真心英雄' in Chinese. It was a challenging task but a very heartwarming experience and the final piece was recorded live in his studio with this amazing video put together to celebrate the experience. This video says it all, how welcoming and kind the JC Action team are and how big of a heart they have! Sharing this moment with the whole team and the participants was a moment I will never forget."

Scan the QR code below to watch the official music video for "Sincere Hero" (真心英雄) by Group Singalong (2023).

The 2nd JCST Action Film Camp is coming in 2024!
Location: Beijing | Date: 13 June 2024 – 24 June 2024

This is your chance to train in the Art of Action Filmmaking with cinema icons of the Jackie Chan Stunt Team. For more than 40 years, the JC Stunt Team has been recognized as one of the most renowned and experienced stunt teams in the world, responsible for some of the most spectacular athletic feats and action scenes in movies such as "Rush Hour", "Police Story", and many others.

As an added bonus, this summer camp is a direct opportunity for the JC Stunt Team to discover new talent. Aspiring stunt performers and action designers will have the chance to showcase their skills and potentially be considered for future projects.

During this training camp, you will have the unique opportunity to learn from true masters of their craft. Not only will the JC Stunt Team teach you the fundamentals of camera ready martial arts and stunt work, they will also share their knowledge and experience in choreographing fight

scenes, and action performance.
Join the JCST for this amazing event and create memories to last a lifetime. Limited spots are available, so don't miss out on this incredible opportunity to train with some of the world's best. The JC Stunt Team looks forward to meeting you!

Picture: Real Jackie Chan Stunt Team vibes during the 2023 camp with Aaron Dexter and Maryline Vo on the Great Wall of China
Note: Closing date for all applications is 15 May, 2024!

How to apply for the 2nd JCST Action Film Camp?

1. Make sure you are 18 and up with a valid passport.
2. Fill out the online application: www.kstarcamps.com/jcstcamp
3. K-STAR and the JC GROUP will go over your application. If you pass this phase they will send you a waiver and a link for online payment.
4. Complete your course payment and submit your waiver with a picture and photo copy of your valid passport.
5. Get a flight landing in Beijing, China (PEK), on June 13th, 2024 (check to see if you need a travel VISA).
6. Send them a copy of your itinerary and that's it!

Your deposit must be received within 72 hours of invoice of your acceptance email in order to secure your spot. Spaces to this event are limited. The remainder of your camp balance must be paid within 90 days of making your deposit or your spot will be passed on to the next person on our waiting list.

Schedule
13 June 2024: Arrival Day PEK
14 June 2024: JC Welcome Day
15 June to 21 June 2024: JC Stunt Training
22 + 23 June 2024: Tourism Day
24 June 2024: Departure Day PEK
Schedule may change.

The next generation is also catered for The Year of the Dragon will also cater for those under 18, with the 2nd JCST Action Film Camp and, for the first time, the JCST Youth Camp taking place one week before the adult version. Get ready for the adventure of a lifetime at the first ever JCST Youth Camp with the Jackie Chan Stunt Team, where action, excitement, and martial arts collide. This extraordinary Camp offers aspiring young artists the opportunity to learn about the art of on screen performance from the best in the business.

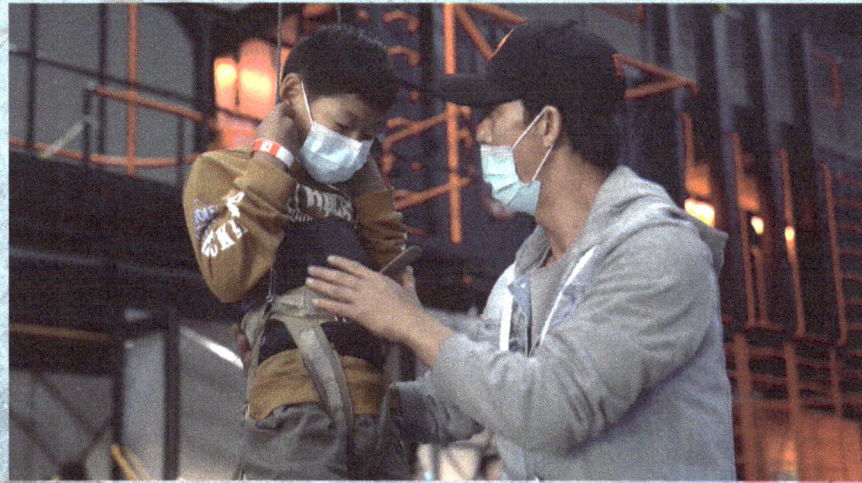

Under the expert guidance of Jackie Chan's legendary stunt team, the trainees will be immersed in the world of exciting stunts, innovative choreography, and martial arts performance. From practicing basic kicks and flips to harnessing their inner courage and discipline, participants will gain invaluable skills while forging lasting friendships in China's capital city of Beijing. In addition to the thrilling stunts and martial arts training, trainees will have the opportunity to explore China's rich history by visiting iconic sites like the Shaolin Temple. Nestled among serene mountains, this ancient Temple is renowned as the birthplace of Zen Buddhism and the cradle of Kung Fu. The trainees will immerse themselves in the spiritual and martial heritage of the Shaolin monks, witnessing their mesmerizing displays of power and agility. This visit will provide a deep appreciation for the historical and cultural roots of martial arts, allowing trainees to connect with the traditions that have inspired Jackie Chan and action cinema. The JC Youth Camp is not only an unforgettable learning experience, but also the chance to build confidence and a lifelong passion for adventure. So, gear up and get ready to join the ranks of fearless stunt performers, all under the watchful eye of the iconic Jackie Chan Stunt Team. Location: Beijing | Date: 3 June 2024 – 13 June 2024 | English translators will be provided

How to apply for the 1st JCST Youth Camp?

Pictures: From 2 to 4 October 2020, an open day was held at the former JCST Action Film Training Center (成家班训练基地) in Tianjin. Under strict corona conditions. Families with children had fun with acrobatics, stretching, stunts and many other activities. Please scan the QR code to watch the full 4K video!

1. Make sure everyone applying for travel has a valid passport.
2. Make sure a parent or guardian fills out our online application: www.kstarcamps.com/jcstyouthcamp
3. Please note, it is mandatory for all minors to be accompanied by an adult.
4. K-STAR and the JC GROUP will go over your application. If you pass this phase they will send you a waiver and a link for online payment.
5. Complete your course payment and submit your waiver with a picture and photo copy of your valid passport.
6. Get a flight landing in Beijing, China (PEK), on June 3rd, 2024 (check to see if you need a VISA)
7. Send them a copy of your itinerary and that's it!

Your deposit must be received within 72 hours of invoice of your acceptance email in order to secure your spot. Spaces to this event are limited. The remainder of your camp balance must be paid within 90 days of making your deposit or your spot will be passed on to the next person on our waiting list.

Schedule
3 June 2024: Arrival Day PEK
4 June to 7 June 2024: JC Stunt Training
8 June 2024: JC Stunt Training & closing ceremony
9 June 2024: Travel to Shaolin Temple
10 June to 12 June 2024: Shaolin Training
13 June 2024: Departure Day PEK
Schedule may change.

Testimonials
The first Jackie Chan Stunt Team Action Camp in 2023 made a lasting impression on the participants. I would like to let some of them have their say here. Thank you for sharing your experiences with us and giving interested martial artists, stunt performers, action actors and filmmakers the opportunity to make an informed decision for their future and career.

Florian Müller
Stuntman, stunt coordinator | Switzerland (www.51stunts.ch)

In spring 2023, a friend told me about the first stunt camp open to the public run by the world-famous Jackie Chan stunt team in Beijing. I immediately dropped everything. Cost? Holiday? Visa? Whatever, I had to act immediately. The day of departure came sooner than expected. I wasn't travelling directly from Zurich to Beijing, but first to Shanghai to visit my family, who I hadn't seen for four years due to the pandemic (my wife is from Shanghai). When we finally arrived at the hotel in Beijing, we went straight to our first dinner together. It's hard to explain, but I immediately sensed a concentrated energy that had come together in the same room with all the camp participants. It felt like the participants came from all corners and countries of the world. On the first day of training, the group marched to the anonymous location of the training centre, protected from the public. The gates opened and we were warmly greeted by Jackie's dogs and familiar faces from the Sing Ga Ban. The camp leader was He Hun from the 5th generation of the stunt team. We practised Wushu, wirework, fight choreography and related reactions, there were some surprises and special guest speakers like Tong Chuan (4th generation), Zac Wang (8th generation) and Perry Ho, Cinematographer from Jackie's team, who shared their unique experiences, gave tips and answered

Florian Müller with 4th generation JCST member Tong Chuan

questions from the participants. Even though Jackie couldn't be there himself as he was busy filming "Project P", it was definitely a priceless experience to learn from and train with such legends. Unfortunately, a training session like this goes by far too quickly and you don't want to go home. But you have to remember why you went there in the first place, to create something yourself, to incorporate what you learnt into your next film project and to make the projects the best possible work of art with the inspiration of Jackie's unique style.

Emilie Guillaume
Actress, martial artist, fight choreographer, tricker, stuntwoman | Belgium (www.emilieguillaume.com)

The first ever Jackie Chan stunt camp was a dream! Like a dream coming true, and like living the dream. I was all along feeling like a kid with my eyes opened and a big smile on my face all the time. If I am what I am today it is because of Jackie Chan, he inspired me so much in what I wanted to do with my life. I've been watching his movies since I was a kid, then became an actress, went to train in China for a little while, to know a bit of the country he came from and specialized in stunt and fighting choreography just to follow his path. When I'm creating a fight scene, he's always in a corner of my head, he's my inspiration! When I heard about that camp, I had to go for it! I mean I couldn't miss this once in a lifetime opportunity! I applied straight away and luckily got accepted! It was a dream to meet people from his team, the most talented people in the world in the industry, to train with them and to be surrounded by participants from all over the world with the same passion about it. Honestly, I cannot even express the feeling because it was so intense! It was just a blast to learn so much from them, to see their generosity to teach and to share their passion. We learnt about physicality a lot, about the precision of the moves, through Wushu and fight choreo classes, we learnt about the filming, the teambuilding and about the team work, the importance of storytelling, about the meaning of each move for the story… We learnt it through their interviews and as well, through the creation of some fighting videos that we had to do as a group and that we debriefed. And most importantly, we learnt about the dedication for their work and why Jackie Chan and his team are really the best of the best! Even if I knew it already of course! Picture: Emilie Guillaume during her recording of the Group Singalong version for "Sincere Hero" (**真心英雄**)

Emilie Guillaume during her recording of the Group Singalong version for "Sincere Hero" (真心英雄)

Arman Ansari
Action performer, stunt coordinator, fight choreographer | Finland (www.armanansari.com)

First of all, there are a million different words on how to describe my experience and feelings from the Jackie Chan Stunt Team Camp 2023. Imagine your biggest dream, which you were only dreaming, suddenly becoming true. It's insane. All my life, since I was seven years old, I've been watching and admiring Jackie Chan and his international worldwide known stunt

team. I knew right away what I wanted from my life. Not to be the next Jackie, but to be an action performer. Every time I watched his movies, I was so impressed by the stuntmen working with him. How they react, fight, and fall. And I wanted to learn that. My dream has always been to meet and work with the Jackie Chan stunt team.

As an action performer and stunt coordinator in a country like Finland where we don't even have action genre movies or a proper stunt course this opportunity meant more than anything to me. And I'm super glad and grateful to be able to have participated in the first JCST Action Camp in Beijing. And to experience the Jackie Chan family hood, see insights, talk with the team, hear their stories, train with them, learn more and new details about Jackie Chan. And spending time in the official Jackie Chan Training Centre!

This is an opportunity for any filmmaker, action/stunt performer, actor etc. to (really) learn about stunts and film fighting. This journey totally changed my values and the way I work. I see things differently now, and I understand the importance of screen writing which helps me with my work as a fight choreographer back home to create unique fighting sequences with the actors in an unfolding story. I'm thankful for Philip Sahagun for organising this event and blessed for the JC Stunt Team for treating me as a family member. If I were you, I wouldn't hesitate to apply. I'll see you at the next camp!

Maryline Vo
Martial artist, stuntwoman, action actress France (@maryline_le on Instagram)

As a true Jackie Chan fan and as a martial artist, my acceptance to go to Beijing to train with the JC STUNT TEAM blew my mind. I was both excited and full of doubts. New in the stunt industry, I felt strangely illegitimate to be part of this adventure. So I have asked myself: "What would Jackie Chan would do?". Of course, he would jump on this opportunity to grow, to train, and to be part of the game. Like Jackie, I am a big kid, I want to play too. My heart was beaten so hard the first day at the camp. I was impressed by all the people around, the infrastructure, and the whole spirit. Everything reminds you of Jackie Chan movies. From the garden to the wall. I thought "this is it; Jackie was there". It gave me such inner strength. The kind of strength that can change you to the core. These 7 days were one of the best of my life. Because it was magical. More than the sweat, more than the action classes the coaches gave to us, it was a revelation. It felt "home". A safe place where each team member can find his place, can grow at his own pace without any judgement. I felt that I can be myself and much more. Fears that paralysed me before progressively disappeared. I felt that I have been seen and understood by the JC STUNT TEAM for who I am, for real. The genuine support and the true passion shared there have the abilities to change you to the best. I left China with a precious gift, the Jackie Chan spirit stronger than ever. So let's play harder! #NeverSayNo Picture: Maryline Vo with 5th generation JCST member He Jun and the famous "Mr. Nice Guy" tire in the background that once and for many years decorated the wall in Jackie's old Hong Kong office

Contact: Philip Sahagun
website: www.philipsahagun.com
Philip Sahagun (YouTube):
www.youtube.com/@PhilipSahagun
K-STAR website: www.kstarcamps.com
Jackie Chan Stunt Camps (Instagram):
www.instagram.com/jcstuntcamp

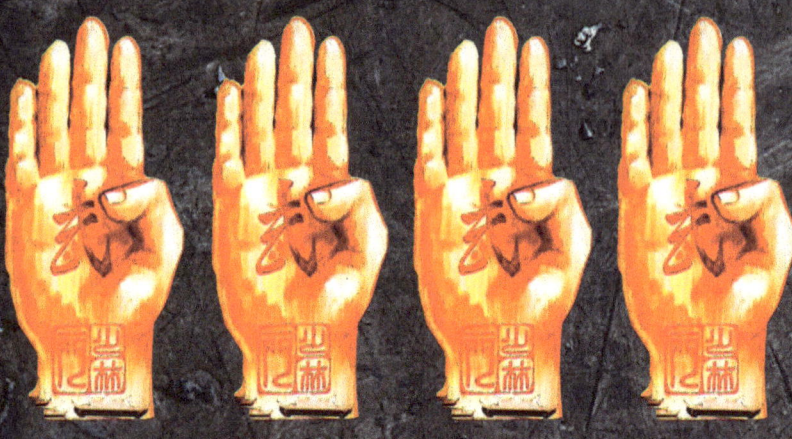

HANDS OF STONE

Jackie Chan's face and hand prints for the professional collector

by Thorsten Boose
December 2023

ARTIST JOSEPH MALARA AND JACKIE CHAN ON THE BALCONY OF THE HILTON HOTEL, MIAMI, FLORIDA, IN AUGUST 1998.

When you have reached the lowest point in your life, there is nowhere to go but up. This is where a person's true character is revealed. In 1994, New York artist Joseph Malara made a virtue of necessity and worked his way up from flea markets to the living rooms of the stars in just a few years with a clever business idea. A true American story.

"Joseph Malara aka "The Artist of The Stars" was the founder of Hands of Stone. He had dreams of opening the first of its kind Museum consisting of those who excelled in their fields. However that Museum unfortunately never opened. This collection took many years, time and out of pocket financing for Malara to create."In his early 30s, Joseph Malara was a successful businessman in New York. As the owner of his own maintenance business, he enjoyed the good times and made the decision to move to Florida permanently. He left the business to a relative in New York.

After a bankruptcy, Malara decided against rebuilding the business. Instead, he borrowed USD 100, set up a table at flea markets and offered his new service: Plaster

Joseph With Jack LaLanne

casts as family keepsakes. Business boomed. Malara was able to pay off his debts, afford a company car and office and actually develop a lucrative business model for plaster casts. His company "Hands Of Stone" was born. What set Malara's work apart from others was quite simply his ingenuity. He developed new techniques that allowed up to ten people

Joseph With Luis Gonzalez

to put their hands into moulds at the same time in the most complicated poses. After only a short time, the blank was ready for further processing. A spectacle for customers and an absolutely individualised memento. "You have to make more out of this," thought the artist. A licence process for handprints of stars and starlets was developed. After

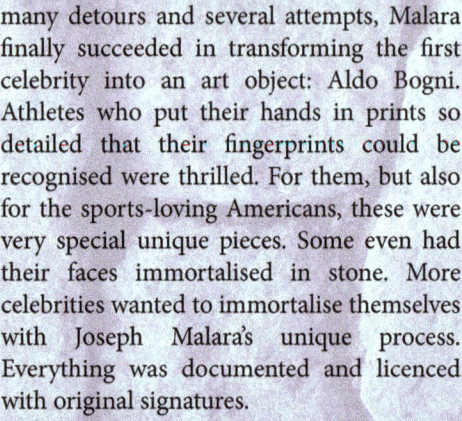
Joseph With Bruce Jenner

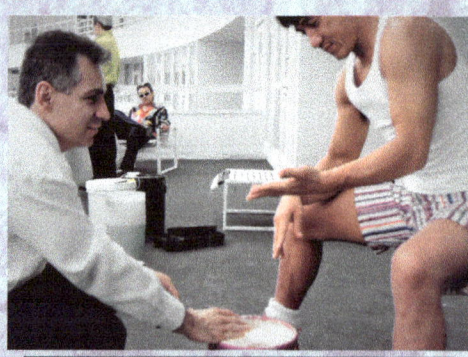

ABOVE: JOSEPH MALARA EXPLAINS TO JACKIE CHAN HOW BEST TO INSERT HIS HAND INTO THE MOULD. AS ALWAYS, WILLIE CHAN WATCHES THE WHOLE THING IN A RELAXED MANNER.

As always, Willie Chan watches the whole thing in a relaxed manner. "I observed in the next room that there was a set up for sparring, like a Dojo. This intrigued me since I had 20 years learning and teaching Mixed Martial Arts and Boxing! I asked Jackie Chan "Can we spar?" He said "Sure!" I thought I was dreaming." In his book, he goes on to tell how Malara and Jackie talked at length about martial arts, Bruce Lee and filmmaking. Jackie was very interested in the artist's method and enthusiastic about how quickly it works. This also appealed to Willie Chan, who knew that

ABOVE IMAGES: FIRST MEETING OF JOSEPH MALARA AND JACKIE CHAN ON 26 NOVEMBER 1997.

many detours and several attempts, Malara finally succeeded in transforming the first celebrity into an art object: Aldo Bogni. Athletes who put their hands in prints so detailed that their fingerprints could be recognised were thrilled. For them, but also for the sports-loving Americans, these were very special unique pieces. Some even had their faces immortalised in stone. More celebrities wanted to immortalise themselves with Joseph Malara's unique process. Everything was documented and licenced with original signatures.

AND THEN ALONG CAME JACKIE CHAN

In his book "Celebrity Sculptures & Hands of Stone, My Story", Joseph Malara writes in several chapters about his encounters with Jackie Chan. At the time of their first meeting, in November 1997, the success of "Rush Hour" (1998) was still a long way off. In fact, Malara and Jackie's manager Willie Chan talked about this new attempt to make it in Hollywood. "By 1997 things started to happen after I had a car accident […] I focused on creating more celebrity hands and faces. I sent letters to those I wanted to meet and immortalize in stone towards my Museum efforts. I got a letter back from Jackie Chan's people; we communicated back then by fax. They have a 13-hour difference in Hong Kong, where Jackie lived. We went back and forth by e-mail or fax until a date was set to meet! We were to meet at a house in Beverly Hills, California."

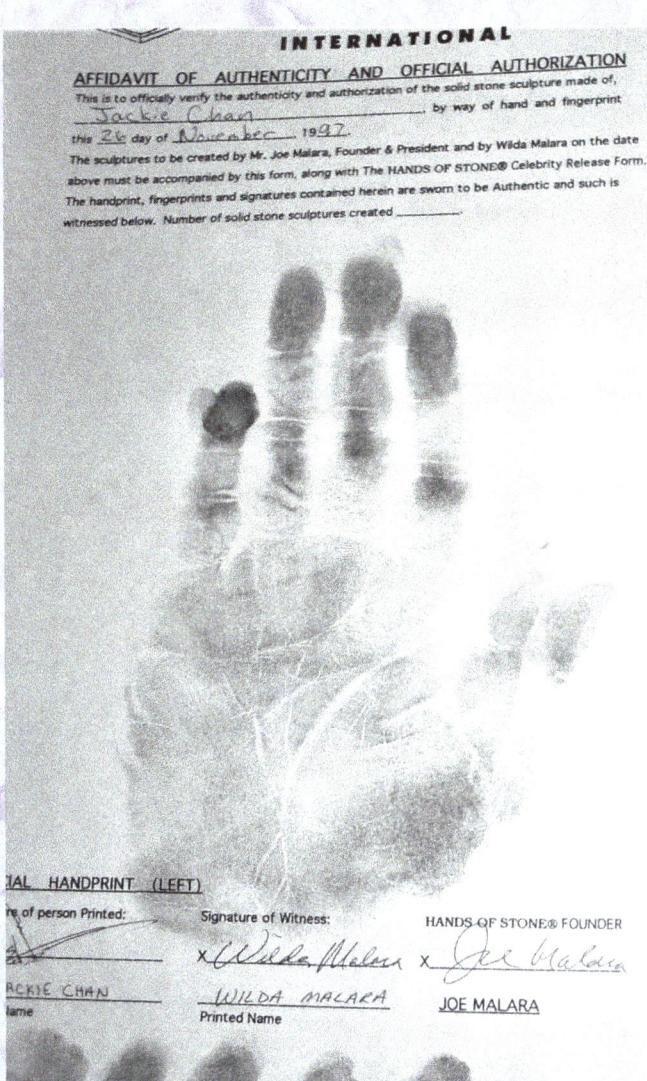
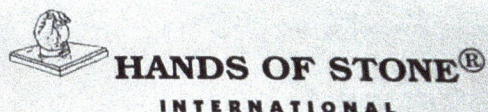

his protégé had very little time at his disposal.

It's one thing for an artist to be able to present their services to one of their own idols and work with them. It's another thing when that star likes the work so much that he commissions more work. The next meeting between Malara and Chan took place nine months later, in August 1998, in the middle of the "Rush Hour" stress. Willie summoned Joseph Malara to the Hilton Hotel in Miami, Florida. As thanks for his prompt acceptance, Jackie presented Joseph with his new autobiography, signed by him. That day, Jackie wanted a very special object: Jackie's hand holding a basketball. While Malara worked out the best way to do it, the two of them talked about films, martial arts and all sorts of other things. Jackie doubled his order and so Malara managed to make the matching trophies for the basketball tournament of the second "Jackie Chan Challenge Cup" in 1998. Even though these two custom-made pieces are not for sale and Joseph Malara was never able to fulfil his dream of having his own Celebrity Sculptures Museum, he still owns original Jackie Chan prints and invites fans of his work to visit his virtual exhibition at www.CelebritySculptures.com.

Jackie Chan's hand and face prints In his book "Celebrity Sculptures & Hands of Stone, My Story", Joseph Malara doesn't just talk about the rosy side of his collaboration with Jackie Chan. There is also some criticism in the artist's lines. If you want to form your own opinion, I highly recommend reading it. Over several pages and in two chapters, he takes the reader on his very personal journey as a struggling yet successful artist of the 90s and 2000s. For the professional collector of memorabilia, the question naturally arises as to whether it is worth investing in an original print of Jackie Chan's hands or face. After all, these are unique pieces that were personally worked on, commissioned and certified by Jackie himself.

Here is a small selection of the items in stock. You can find more items at www.CelebritySculptures.com

JACKIE CHAN BRONZE FACE [$5,399]

Jackie Chan Fist – Light Gold ($1,999)

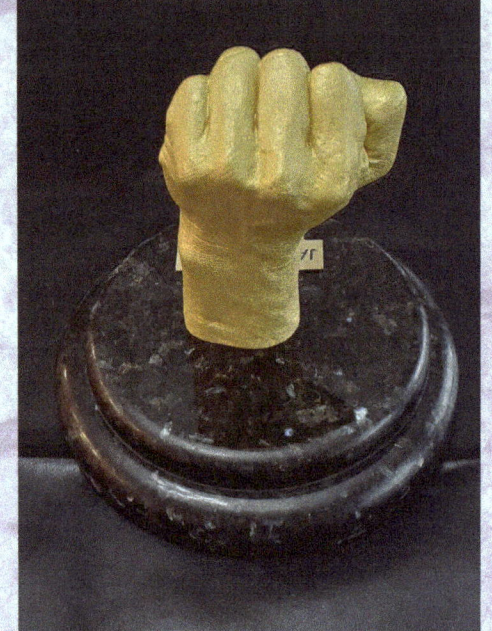

Jackie Chan Peace – Silver Right ($3,999)

The cheapest object offered by Joseph Malara is Jackie's right hand with a thumb up in gold. At 1400 USD, this is still a hefty sum, you might think. But I was able to negotiate a deal with Joseph for the readers of this article: Each item can be purchased directly from the artist at a 10% discount if you quote "HANDS OF STONE" when placing your order in the current calendar year of 2024. Of course, Joseph Malara will also include a signed copy of "Celebrity Sculptures & Hands of Stone, My Story".

Contact the Artist

Joseph Malara
Website: *www.celebritysculptures.com*
E-mail: *JosephMalara@yahoo.com*
Facebook: *www.facebook.com/celebritysculptures*

Disclaimer: The author of this article, Thorsten Boose, as well as Eastern Heroes and the publisher, Ricky Baker, are not affiliated with and do not profit from the sale of objects by the artist Joseph Malara.

THE WONDER OF
SHANGHAI NOON
BY CHRIS GRANT

'It's the Wild Wild West (when I roll into the) Wild Wild West (when I stroll into the) Wild Wild West (when I bounce into the) Wild Wild West...' (Will Smith, Wild Wild West, Theme Song)

I always find my love for Jackie Chan films fascinating. None of my friends cared for these movies, a ferocious passion of mine that my Dad dutifully nurtured. He, of course, became a fan. This was enough for me, I only ever sought his approval and he would listen to me talking up my passion for as long as was possible for any human to bear. I genuinely had no idea how big a star Jackie was in those glorious pre-internet days. Any information about him, his films and general

in 1997. After the incredible success of Brett Ratner's *Rush Hour* Chan became a household name in Britain. I was 18 years old when *Rush Hour* was released, it's a moment I remember well as it was the first time I watched my cinematic hero on the big screen. Suddenly, Jackie Chan was everywhere and a wave of his work became readily available. It was such a special time for a movie obsessive like myself, I went to see Rush Hour in the cinema more times than I can remember and I recall a distinct thought. It isn't possible for a star of this magnitude to be a one hit wonder; too talented and he was absolutely perfect for the American market. I didn't want to see a direct sequel to Rush Hour at that point honestly, although it was justifiably coming, I wanted to see something completely different.

developments was challenging to come by. I remember reading about *Rumble in the Bronx* in 1994 and waiting diligently for the release to the video market

And so, Shanghai Noon was announced. Jackie Chan was heading to the Wild West. I am a massive fan of the Western genre. If I remade High Noon, I would absolutely cast Jackie Chan as Gary Cooper. Frankly, if I made a Star Trek movie I would happily cast Jackie Chan as the enterprise! There was no doubt in my mind that I was soon to witness another perfect cowboy on screen. Shanghai Noon felt fresh and different. The story grabbed me, and the comedic aspects of the film worked splendidly. There was something refreshing about watching Jackie Chan's Chon Wang and his partner Owen Wilson's Roy O'Bannon, going back and forth in a gentle and oddly positive way. The movie was a rip-roaring action adventure that perfectly combined Hollywood flair with Chan's trade mark comedy and astonishing action sequences. Shanghai Noon follows all the usual buddy-buddy movie steps; a relationship between two people that begins antagonistically before flourishing into friendship and respect. Despite the paint by number elements this film elevates itself due to the tremendous writing, the trade mark action and the surprisingly effective acting. Watching Roy O'Bannon and Chon Wang get ludicrously drunk in a bathtub together will forever be pure cinematic joy. It is really something to think that Jackie Chan has brought the world near perfect entertainment for six decades. Seeing the megastar in any project always takes me back to my childhood, i mean really, is anything as special as that? I recently became a father myself, and in such an intense time of joy and wonder I can see why my Dad so diligently nourished my film obsession. I hope to do the same, and when my beautiful daughter asks me about the western genre and where to start I'll give her 5 titles; *Once Upon a time in the West*, *High Noon*, *The Wild Bunch*, *Rio Bravo*, *Go West* and *Jackie Chan's Shanghai Noon*.

JACKIE CHAN FANCLUBS

BY MICHAEL NESBITT

The very first Jackie Chan Fan Club I was introduced to was over 35 years ago, way back in the late 1980s, when I saw an advert in the British Martial Arts Magazine, Combat. The advertisement was for the first ever UK Jackie Chan Fan Club. At the time, I was more of a fan of Bruce Lee's, but only a few years previously I had started hiring out the VPD released Jackie Chan movies from video stores, and instantly fell in love with them. Like most teenagers around that time, I would scour the video rental shops in the hope of finding a Jackie Chan movie I had not seen before. So when I saw the article for the forthcoming JCFC (Jackie Chan Fan Club), in the December 1988 issue of Combat Magazine, I was instantly excited for what was to come. At the same time, the same people running the JCFC were advertising a Fan Club for Bruce Lee, called Bruce Lee and Friends. The Bruce Lee Fan Club never materialised until the mid-90s, however, I did join the Jackie Chan Fan Club. As most people who are old enough to know, these pre-Internet days were tough times, and fans of any genre, were constantly looking for ways to find out any and all information on their favourites. So when a Fan Club would pop up, hundreds or maybe even thousands of people would join, in the hopes of receiving any latest news on their heroes. The newsletters and fanzines we received became a life line for a lot of people, and would brighten up a fans day.

Of course, the 1988 UK Jackie Chan Fan Club was not the first Fan Club to appear, that privileged went to the Japanese. Jackie had been super popular in Japan since the early 1980s. By the 80s, Bruce Lee fans had slowly shifted their alliance to Jackie Chan, mainly due to no new Bruce Lee material being released, and the fact that Jackie was releasing at least one new movie a year. Jackie's style of fighting, combined with his onscreen charisma, made him a Superstar all over Asia. Japan led the way in releasing all kinds of Jackie Chan memorabilia, from records and cassettes, to videos and posters, and host of other items that would become very collectible. They would plaster Jackie's face over anything they could, badges, pencil cases, toys, and even cereal boxes, so it was inevitable that Jackie Chans fame would eventually reach the western audience. By now it was the mid to late 1990s, and the birth of the internet became something of a double edged sword. Now with the internet being so accessible to everyone, it gave you instant access to unlimited photos, footage and information on Jackie, meaning there was no need for Fan Clubs, destroying them by the time the millennium hit. But for those that are old enough to remember, the days of the Fan Clubs are remembered with fond memories, so let's take a look back at some of those Jackie Chan Fan Clubs.

1980-1983 - The Great Dragons

By the late 1970s, Bruce Lee's fan base wasn't as popular as it was earlier in the decade, mainly due to the lack of new material being released. However, there was hope on the horizon, as a new star was becoming more popular, Jackie Chan. Jackie's stardom had begun its steady rise to fame due to the two movies he released in the late 1970s, Snake in the Eagles Shadow, and Drunken

Master, but in the eyes of many he was still wasn't on the same level as Bruce Lee. Dragon, the Japanese Bruce Lee Fan Club, were toying with the idea of starting up a Jackie Chan Fan Club, but, they were worried that he wasn't famous enough to make it a success, so they came up with the idea of doing a Fan Club called, The Great Dragons Fan Club, aka The Bruce Lee and Jackie Chan Fan Club. Like most Fan Cubs, when you joined, you got a membership card, letter, sticker, and the new Great Dragons fanzine. The fanzine always depicted photos of both Bruce and Jackie on the front and back, and for the first 24 issues it was a typical sized fanzine, with a couple of issues having a full colour cover. From issue 25 to 36, the fanzine was exactly the same; however they had

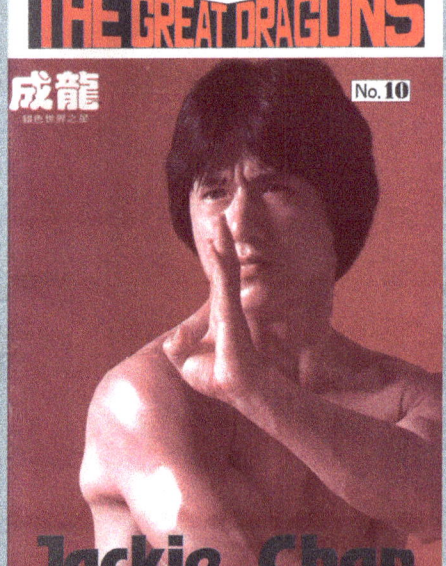

resized it down to an A5 size. After that, the popularity of the club began to dwindle, and it became more of newsletter style fanzine, which looked less polished, and was in black and white. By 1983, the team had decided to close the Fan Club down and solely dedicate a new Fan Club to Jackie Chan; the new club would be called the Jackie Chan Cine Club.

1982-1999
The International Jackie Chan Fan Club

The International Jackie Chan Fan Club which was endorsed by Jackie himself and was run by Jackie's manager Willie Chan, began in July 1982, and was not only the first Jackie Chan Fan Club in Hong Kong, but is considered by many to be the best Jackie Chan Fan Club. Considering it was run by Jackie's manager, all the information you were getting was first hand and up-to-date. It was professionally run, with fans from all over the world joining. Along with the fanzine, you got a membership card and many extras. You would get regular Christmas cards, signed photos, keyrings,

stickers, and a host of other memorabilia. The first 19 issues of the fanzines in black and white, with issue 20 (November 1985) being the first to have a full colour cover. It was only from issue 27 that they included colour pages on the inside. One of the highlights of the bi-monthly magazine that was also printed in both English and Japanese was the amount of rare and new photos that they included. It even had a dedicated section for questions that Jackie would answer himself. The first

membership pack included the membership card, badge, a letter from Jackie, and a signed photo. The Fan Club was one of the longest running Fan Clubs dedicated to Jackie, and shut up shop with the birth of the internet in the spring of 1999. A total of 68 issues of the Fan Club magazine were released. However, the Japanese office of the Official Fan Club did continue for a while after, with a shortened edition of the magazine which was released only in Japan, which was called the "Tokyo Mini News". Even though this was still sanctioned by the Jackie Chan Group, Willie Chan was not involved with the club.

1983-1984 - The Jackie Chan Cine Club

With the dissolution of the Great Dragons Japanese Fan Club, the Jackie Chan Cine Club began with its first fanzine being sent out in October 1983. The Fan Club was not the success it was hoped it would be, and without the added information on Bruce Lee, they lasted only for one year. Jackie's success, specifically in Japan, had not reached its peak at this point, and membership to the Fan Club was not as good as the Great Dragons

Fan Club, so the Club to the decision to shut down in 1984 after 12 fanzines (one issue was a double issue). The fanzine was of the same high quality as the Great Dragons Fan Club, and had a lot of information and photos of Jackie; it also had a lot of interesting content from fans. Issue 1 came with three free Jackie Chan photos, issue 2 came with a free Jackie Chan Sticker, and issue 3 came with a free Jackie Chan Catalogue. However, Jackie Chan fans would not be disappointed as there were a lot more Fan Clubs on the horizon.

成龍

JACKIE CHAN KAIHOO SEARON

jcc JACKIE CHAN CINE CLUB

●編集/発行
ジャッキー・チェン・シネクラブ
〒174 東京都板橋区宮本町62-3
☎03(967)7280

6月1日 第3号

一招半式闘江湖
ジャッキー・チェン

特報

『カンニングモンキー 天中拳』公開

●JC来日グラフ 第2弾
●香港取材

天中拳

"俺たちゃなぁ、少林寺の裏街道をゆくドジで、オバカで、ええカッコしい、いわば天下の人気者だぁ"

極めつけは、必笑座頭天中拳。ぐおわはまだもんね。「蛇拳」なんかズンズンズンハラッとしちゃう。「笑拳」だってバキッ ビシッ。「酔拳」よりもドキッ

成龍

JACKIE CHAN
KAIHOO
SEARON

jcc
JACKIE CHAN CINE CLUB
●編集/発行
ジャッキー・チェン・シネクラブ
〒174 東京都板橋区宮本町62-3
☎ 03(967)7280
8月1日 第5号

天中拳 全ハイライト

● クンフー教室
●● 香港パーティ取材
● フリー・スペース

成龍 JACKIE CHAN KAIHOO SEARON

JACKIE CHAN CINE CLUB

●編集/発行
ジャッキー・チエン・シネクラブ
〒174 東京都板橋区宮本町62-3
☎ 03 (967) 7280

10月1日 第7号

「成龍拳」公開日決定！
クンフー教室④ 武器編
●フリースペース
●イラストコーナー
●JCC情報局

成龍

JACKIE CHAN KAIHOO SEARON

jcc JACKIE CHAN CINE CLUB

●編集／発行
ジャッキー・チェン・シネクラブ
〒174 東京都板橋区宮本町62-3
☎ 03 (967) 7 2 8 0

1月　第10・11合併号

JC新作フィルムハイライト

プロジェクトA
五福星

マンガ新連載1
『龍と鳳』

1983-1984 – The Jackie Chan Cinema Club

This Fan Club was another short lived Jackie Chan Fan Club that didn't even last a whole year. It released only 4 black and white fanzines called the Cinema Fan, but with far superior Fan Clubs already in operation, the club couldn't compete.

1985 – The Jackie Chan Joint Club (JJC)

This Japanese Fan Club is a bit of a strange one. The first bulletin/newsletter was released in May 1985 and was more dedicated to the selling of Jackie Chan memorabilia. The bulletin was mainly made up of Jackie merchandise for sale, and over the next few months it was in operation, the team behind the club couldn't decide if it should be a Fan Club dedicated solely to Jackie, or Jackie memorabilia, as they constantly asked fans to send in artwork, poems, letters and so on, so they could start up a regular fanzine. This however, didn't materialise, and with only three bulletins/newsletters being released, it finally closed down. Along with the membership card, and three newsletters, they sent out a number of price lists with Jackie Chan memorabilia on them, but nothing more substantial than that.

JJC速報版 NO3

ジャッキー・チェン=ジョイントクラブ

龍兄虎弟《神のよろい》完成迫る
9月上映予定

日本中のJCファンに衝撃を与えた9月7日の事故以来中断されていたユーゴロケもいよいよ完成！

探険家"アジアの鷹"に扮するジャッキー、女殺し屋集団、邪教組織を相手にジャッキー・カンフーが爆裂!!

《ベオグラード発14日AP》の外電が入ったのが9月15日、日本中のジャッキーファンが大騒ぎ……。1ヶ月近く正確な情報が入らずファンをヤキモキさせたことを思い出します。事故当日撮影の"龍兄虎弟〜神のよろい"も撮影地ユーゴが雪の季節に入り必然的に一時中断となった。屋外ロケが多く、春にクランク・インして秋にクランク・アップするならそれほど困らないけど、間に冬が入ると最低半年は待機しなければならない。
サモボルは、城壁から木へ飛び移り、坂を滑り降りるアクション・シーンに失敗して大手術を受けてた悪夢の地。手術のために剃った髪の毛も、もとに戻らないことや撮影条件が変わってしまうことで今春まで順延されていた"龍兄虎弟"も5月30日ユーゴスラビアのロケを終了。
空路パリへ飛びクライマックス・シーンの撮影を済ませ、いよいよ香港での編集作業に入っている。日本公開予定は9月。
ストーリーは、探険家"アジアの鷹"に扮するジャッキーが聖書に記録された6つの神器をめぐって暗躍する邪教集団の世界制覇を阻止して、恋人や親友を救出するという簡単なストーリー。ジャッキーは、映画は、観せることノ、に重点をおいている。内容、ストーリーは、単純明解にして誰にでも理解しやすく組立てをし、最大のポイントは、アクション!!においている。
"龍兄虎弟"のクライマックスは、空中シーン、ジェット機から気球、気球から地上への飛び降りシーンは、ドギモを抜かれる。女にヨワイ!?ジャッキーが4人の女殺し屋と戦う蹴りの応酬は見もの。

お詫びとお知らせ

JJCニュース3号の発行が遅れてすみませんでした。理由は、いっぱいありますが言いわけをせず次回から遅れたりせず努力します。次号の予定は、プロジェクトAパートⅡ〈仮題〉の情報が会員のみなさまからの原稿が沢山集まった時は、JJCニュース〈タブロイド版の新聞〉になります。

"龍兄虎弟"スチール写真アルバムセット予約受付のご案内

特製バッヂ＋チラシ下敷＋スチール写真アルバム
特別セット価格　1セット2,000円《送料サービス》

スチール写真アルバムは、手作りのオリジナル商品です。注文を受けてから制作するため、いつもお届けが遅くなってご迷惑をおかけしています。今回は、このようなことのないように予約で受け付けて映画上映前に皆様の手元に届くように企画しました。

近況

ジャッキーは次回作プロジェクトAパートⅡの撮影計画に入っている。事故以来初めての本格的アクション映画へのチャレンジだ！又、新しいジャッキーをファンの皆んなに見せてくれることだろう。期待しよう！

新会員証発行のお知らせ

デザインは変わりませんが、ラミネート加工した新しい会員証を再発行しております。新しい会員証を希望される方は製作費100円＋送料60円とあなたの会員No.を記入してお申し込み下さい。

《JJC》では原稿を募集してま〜す………。
近い将来JJCの会報を作りたいと計画しております。皆さんも会報作りに参加して下さい。文通、作詩、イラスト、映画評、ジャッキー評、スナップなどお寄せ下さい。

《JJC》ジャッキー・チェン=ジョイント・クラブ

ジャッキー・チェン＝ジョイントクラブ
JJC速報版 新製品案内 NO 号外

アイドル掛時計
直径22cmのブラック・フレームに
文字版は写真入り、
定価4800円を
2880円の特別価格で限定販売

新発売

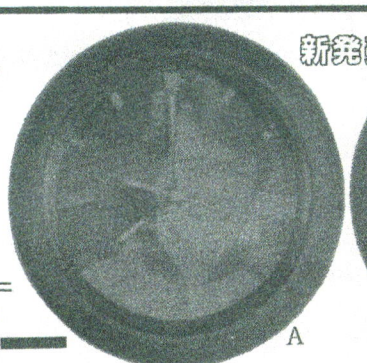
A

B

1989年カレンダー
1本1500円+送料は何本でも1回に付600円 別送料

スタンド・カレンダー
1枚500円
+送料は何枚でも1回に付400円

A   B

女の子の必需品

ブラック・ボディーの角型コンパクト
1個800円
+送料は何個でも1回に付400円

ゴールドフレームの丸型コンパクト
1個800円
+送料は何個でも1回に付400円

女性なら誰でも持っていあるコンパクト（両面鏡）にジャッキーの写真を樹脂コーティングした貴女だけのオリジナル・コンパクトです。

アイドル手帳〈バインダー式〉

1冊2500円+送料は何冊でも1回に付400円
今年からオリジナル・ラミカードの裏面は1989年のカレンダー付です。

※オリジナル・ラミカード+デジタル時計付ボールペンがセットされています。
※色は赤と黒があります。希望する色を記入して下さい。
※この手帳は東京メールショップのオリジナルです。レザータイプの高級ビニール製で、ラミカードやテレホンカードを入れるポケットとシャープペン又はボールペンが付くようになっています。中の用紙はメモとアドレスと時間表がセットされています。

最新木製パネル　1枚1,000円+送料400円

A B D H I K L M N O P Q
R S T U V W X Y Z 1 2 3
4 5 6 7 8 9 10 11 12 13

カレンダー以外の商品の送料は1回に付400円です。カレンダーだけは送料が別にかかり

シャッキー・チェン＊特別カタログ

このカタログはジャッキー・チェン＊ジョイントクラブの皆様とJCファンに送る特別カタログです。

このカタログに掲載されている商品は、一部の商品を除き全て半額です。

8ミリ・フィルムと功夫服装用品のシャツ・ズボン・ユニホームは特別価格です。
ポスターの料金は半額になりますが、送料は何本でも1回に付600円です。
カラーピンナップの料金は半額になりますが、木製パネルの料金は割引になりません。

申し込み方法

ご注意
①申し込みの時は、必ず下記のJC商品半額割引券を添付して下さい。
②こんかいはJJC会員の為に特別に企画したイベントなので代金の支払い方法は全て前払いとなります。
（どうしても後払いで、と云う人は申し込み金として1000円だけ先に送ってください、前払い注文の方の発送がすみしだい発送します。多少の時間が掛かるかもしれませんのでご了承下さい。
③送料（発送手数料）は北海道、九州、沖縄地区の方は1回に付800円、北海道、九州、沖縄地区以外の方は1回に付600円となりますので注文金額の合計にこの送料分を加算してお申し込み下さい。

BRUCE LEE / JACKIE CHAN KUNGFU MAGAZINES 《李小龍＆成龍 武学書刊》

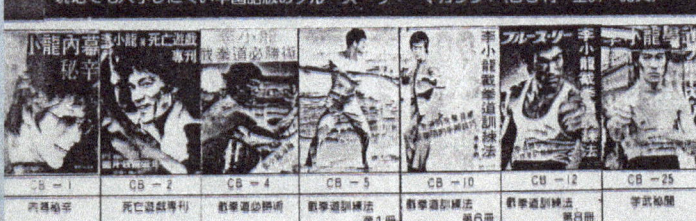

BRUCE LEE MAGAZINES

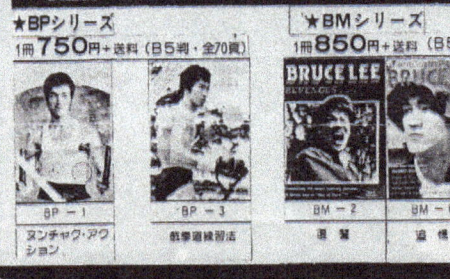

香港製(中国語版) 功夫雑誌 KUNGFU MAGAZINES　1冊650円＋送料

カラーブロマイド　1枚200円

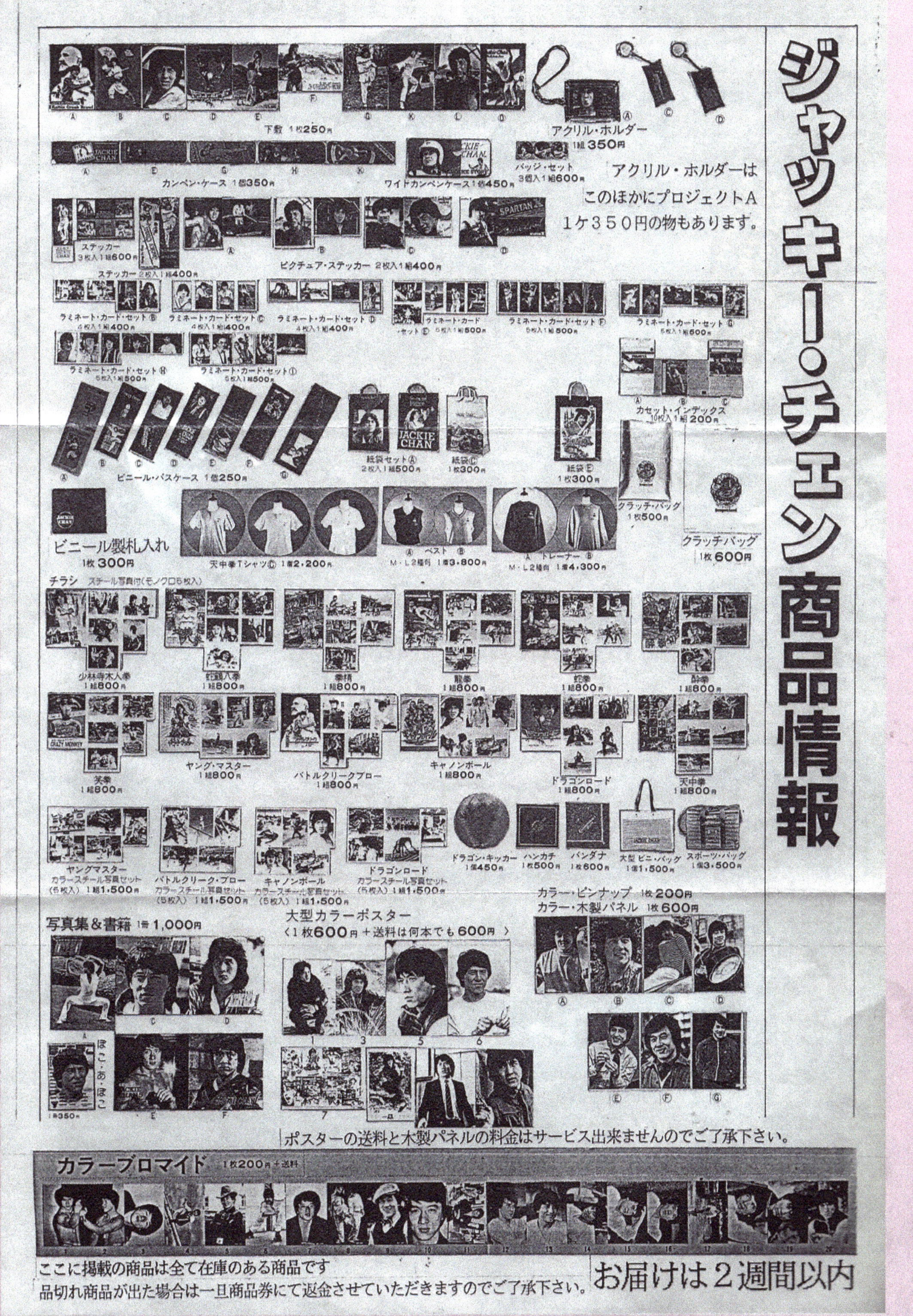
ジャッキー・チェン商品情報
下敷 1枚250円
アクリル・ホルダー 1組350円
カンペン・ケース 1個350円
ワイドカンペンケース 1個450円
バッジ・セット 3個入1組600円
アクリル・ホルダーは このほかにプロジェクトA 1ケ350円の物もあります。
ステッカー 3枚入1組600円
ステッカー 2枚入1組400円
ピクチュア・ステッカー 2枚入1組400円
ラミネート・カード・セットⒷ 4枚入1組400円
ラミネート・カード・セットⒸ 4枚入1組400円
ラミネート・カード・セットⒹ 4枚入1組400円
ラミネート・カード・セットⒺ 5枚入1組500円
ラミネート・カード・セットⒻ 5枚入1組500円
ラミネート・カード・セットⒼ 5枚入1組600円
ラミネート・カード・セットⒽ 5枚入1組500円
ラミネート・カード・セットⒾ 5枚入1組500円
カセット・インデックス 10枚入1組200円
ビニール・パスケース 1個250円
紙袋セットⒶ 2枚入1組500円
紙袋Ⓒ 1枚300円
紙袋Ⓔ 1枚300円
クラッチ・バッグ 1枚500円
ビニール製札入れ 1枚300円
天中拳Tシャツ© 1着2,200円
ベスト M・L2種有 1着3,800円
トレーナー M・L2種有 1着4,300円
クラッチバッグ 1枚600円
チラシ スチール写真付(モノクロ5枚入)
少林寺木人拳 1組800円
蛇鶴八拳 1組800円
拳精 1組800円
龍拳 1組800円
蛇拳 1組800円
酔拳 1組800円
笑拳 1組800円
ヤング・マスター 1組800円
バトルクリークブロー 1組800円
キャノンボール 1組800円
ドラゴンロード 1組800円
天中拳 1組800円
ヤングマスター カラースチール写真セット (5枚入) 1組1,500円
バトルクリーク・ブロー カラースチール写真セット (5枚入) 1組1,500円
キャノンボール カラースチール写真セット (5枚入) 1組1,500円
ドラゴンロード カラースチール写真セット (5枚入) 1組1,500円
ドラゴン・キッカー 1個450円
ハンカチ 1枚500円
バンダナ 1枚600円
大型ビニ・バッグ 1個1,500円
スポーツ・バッグ 1個3,500円
写真集&書籍 1冊1,000円
大型カラーポスター 〈1枚600円+送料は何本でも600円〉
カラー・ピンナップ 1枚200円
カラー・木製パネル 1枚600円
ぽこ・あ・ぽこ ¥350
ポスターの送料と木製パネルの料金はサービス出来ませんのでご了承下さい。
カラーブロマイド 1枚200円+送料
ここに掲載の商品は全て在庫のある商品です
品切れ商品が出た場合は一旦商品券にて返金させていただきますのでご了承下さい。
お届けは2週間以内

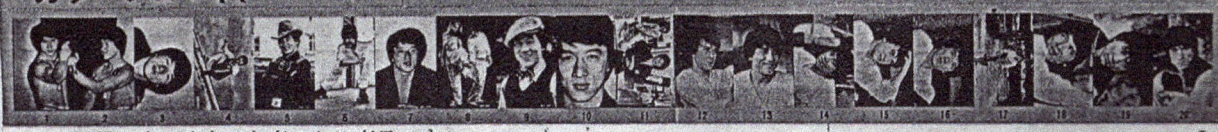

1989-1990 – The Jackie Chan Fan Club (JCFC)

The JCFC has the distinction of being the first ever Jackie Chan Fan Club in the UK. Founded in 1988, the Fan Club was run by Ricky Baker and Chris Alexis, who were the Directors of the club. The President was Bey Logan, with the Vice President being Dean Jones. This was for me the one and only Jackie Chan Fan Club as this was the first one I ever joined. On joining, you received your membership pack, which consisted of the first newsletters, poster, and membership card, all housed in a bright yellow folder. By issue 4, the newsletter was changed into a fanzine, with the last issue being number 7. Afterwards it was decided that the Fan Club would morph into Eastern Heroes, a magazine that still continues to this day. The great thing about the JCFC was the film shows they put on at the Scala Cinema in Kings Cross, London, and the multiple catalogues they released, advertising rare magazine, books, posters, and VHS videos.

J.C.F.C. MERCHANDISE LIST

MARTIAL ARTS MOVIES (Vol.1)
47 Trailers 2 hrs long approx inc EASTERN CONDORS, SHANGHAI SHANGHAI, WALK ON FIRE, EYES OF THE DRAGON, MIRACLE, ROSA, ZU WARRIOR, LINE OF DUTY 3, MIRACLE FIGHTERS and PROUD AND CONFIDENT. Just a few of the Non Stop Action Fight Scenes available, everything the Martial Arts Movie fan wants on one tape ...... ONLY £15.00

MARTIAL ARTS MOVIE TRAILERS (Vol.2) NEW
50 Trailers of Non Stop Action inc LINE OF DUTY 4, FORTUNE CODE (Samo Hung Andy Lau) ANGLE 3 (Moon Lee), CITY COPS (Cynthia Rothrock), CHINESE GODS, "BRUCE LEE CARTOON", SHANGHAI EXPRESS (Cynthia Rothrock, Samo Hung) BETTER TOMORROW PART 1 (Chow Yuen Fat, Ti Lung) DRAGON FAMILY (Andy Lau, Alan Tau), PRODIGAL SON (Yuen Biao, Samo Hung), FIRST MISSION (Jackie Chan - uncut version extra fight scenes), CRIMINAL HUNTER (Dick Wei), OPERATION PINK SQUAD (Femme Fatale action), MAGIC CRYSTAL (Cynthia Rothrock, Andy Lau), plus loads more ... have a glimpse at the movies you thought you would never see ... ONLY £15.00

VIDEO IMPORTS

PAINTED FACES You've read the review, now see the movie. This semi auto-biographical account on the life of Jackie Chan, Samo Hung and Yuen Biao as they grow up inside a Peking Opera School. Excellent quality - Chinese - with English subs .. £20.00
Stars Samo Hung and Lam Chan Ying .. <u>Not to be missed</u>

THE PROTECTOR Chinese version with many scenes not available in U.K. print, a must for the collector. Now for a limited period ... ONLY £15.00

POLICE STORY Chinese version with over 20 mins extra. Never before screened in U.K. See the famous pencil scene, plus loads of extra footage. Shot on 3/4 screen with English subtitles. Rare collectors. ONLY £20.00

CYNTHIA ROTHROCK TRAILER TAPE A selection of scenes from Cynthia's movies, inc. CITY COPS, MAGIC CRYSTAL, SHANGHAI EXPRESS, EYES OF THE DRAGON plus much more, also highlights of Cynthia's visit to England ... ONLY £9.99

CYNTHIA IN THE U.K. Highlights from Cynthia's U.K. visit in Dec. 89. Shows Cindy talking at Cheungs Restaurant, plus highlights from Scala Cinema show. Also some highlights from when Cindy did a special 2 hour seminar. A must for Rothrock fans ... ONLY £20.00 (Free Cynthia poster)

(All videos £1.25 P&P inc recorded delivery)

AUDIO CASSETTES

ARMOUR OF GOD	Sound track	£4.00
YOUNG MASTER	Sound track	£4.00
THE PROTECTOR	Sound track	£4.00
THE BIG BRAWL	Sound track	£4.00
JACKIE SINGS HIS FAVOURITE SONGS (TRADITIONS)		£6.00
BRUCE LEE: MY WAY OF KUNG FU inc extract with Bruce actually talking - a must for Lee fans		£5.00

(All cassettes 50p P&P)

BRUCE LEE T/SHIRT (by Jerry Poteet)
Specially commissioned shirt, not available any more, shows Bruce Lee in Logo form with Jeet-Keen-Do and Jerry Poteet, writen around the top half of Bruce's body. Logo is situated over left side of chest. T/Shirts are high quality and come in red or black, medium or large (there are only a few shirts left) and they have now become collectors' pieces. Usually £11.95 now only £5.95 + 75p P&P

SHAOLIN TEMPLE (the movie) NOW THE BOOK
Jet Lee is now fast becoming one of the new talents in the movie world yet early in the 80s Jet produced a trilogy of movies centred around Shaolin Temple, and demonstrating the elegant but powerful style of Wu-Shu. We now have a limited amount of this souvenir booklet (50 pages) in full colour highlighting scenes from the movie, also a background on this multi-talented martial artist.
Collector item ... ONLY £2.95 Free P&P

JACKIE CHAN STICKERS 6 stickers for £1.00

JACKIE CHAN FAN CLUB Newsletters 1.2.3. There are now only a few of these packages left, smartly bound in yellow J.C.F.C. folder complete with poster. These will not be <u>reprinted</u> and are fast rising in value. If you require one of these sets then please send off soon. <u>THIS IS THE LAST OFFER</u>
ONLY £15.00 Free P&P

MERCHANDISE LIST

JACKIE PORTRAIT BY DEAN JONES FROM ISSUE NO. 7	£ 1.00 EACH
NEWSLETTER BACK ISSUES 1, 2, 3 (ONLY ONE PER PERSON) INCLUDING FOLDER	£ 8.00 PER SET
BIG BRAWL POSTER (SPECIAL OFFER) WERE £2.95 EACH	
SCALA CINEMA POSTER (SPECIAL OFFER) NOW ONLY	£ 1.50 EACH
J.C. FOLDER (SPECIAL OFFER) WAS £2.95 NOW (ONLY ONE PER PERSON)	£ 2.00
J.C. NEWSLETTER NO. 4 (16 PAGE B/W INCL. MIRACLE REVIEW/HAND OF DEATH)	£ 2.50
AUDIO SOUNDTRACKS - YOUNG MASTER	£ 5.00
PROTECTOR	£ 5.00
BIG BRAWL	£ 5.00
ARMOUR OF GOD	£ 5.00
SPECIAL XMAS OFFER ALL FOUR FOR	£18.00
THE PROTECTOR - LIMITED POSTER, FULL COLOUR A2. PICTURE SHOWS MULTIPLE SHOTS	£ 2.50
ARMOUR OF GOD - LIMITED POSTER, FULL COLOUR A2. JACKIE WITH CROSSBOW.	£ 2.50
FEARLESS HYENA PART II (ENGLISH)	£19.95
SPIRITUAL KUNG FU	£19.95
CHAN BEHIND THE SCENES VIDEO DOCUMENTARY (60 MINS APPROX) 1 HOUR	£20.00
HAND OF DEATH VIDEO - ENGLISH VERSION	£25.00
NEW POSTER, A3 COLOUR, MIRACLE	£ 5.00
BRUCE LEE TRANSFERS - SET OF 6 DIFFERENT POSES, FULL SIZE FOR T/SHIRTS. LIMITED.	£ 4.95 SET PER

WE ALSO HAVE A RANGE OF STILLS, FULL COLOUR, LAMINATED, A3 SIZE UNFORTUNATELY, WE DO NOT HAVE SPACE TO SHOW YOU THE PICTURES BUT A DESCRIPTION IS OFFERED TO HELP YOU CHOOSE. STILLS ARE LIMITED AND COST £7.50 EACH. ALL STILLS ARE EXCEPTIONALLY RARE.

PAINTED FACES - STILL SHOWS POSTER ADVERTISEMENT
EASTERN CONDORS - STILL SHOWS POSTER ADVERTISEMENT
HALF A LOAF OF KUNG FU - MULTI SHOTS FROM MOVIE
REVENGE OF DRUNKEN MASTER - POSTER ADVERT, JACKIE WITH VASE
REVENGE OF DRUNKEN MASTER - SYNOPSIS + PHOTOS
FILM SHOW POSTER, NOV 27TH 1988. ARTWORK BY DEAN JONES. SUPERB COLOUR ILLUSTRATION - EASTERN CONDORS, PROJECT A II, DRAGONS FOREVER.
THE PROTECTOR - AMERICAN POSTER WITH PHOTOGRAPHIC PICTURES
SNAKE IN EAGLES SHADOW - JACKIE
SNAKE IN EAGLES SHADOW - JACKIE IN TRAINING
SNAKE IN EAGLES SHADOW - JACKIE IN BATTLE
DRAGON LORD - JACKIE CLIMBING HUMAN PYRAMID
JACKIE 1 - A2 FULL COLOUR POSTER - JACKIE IN HALF BODY SHOT IN KUNG FU POSE - £5.00
JACKIE 2 - A2 FULL COLOUR POSTER - JACKIE IN SECOND HALF BODY SHOT - £5.00

PLEASE ALLOW 28 DAYS WHEN ORDERING, AS IF A PRODUCT SELLS OUT, WE DO TRY TO RE-ORDER SO AS NOT TO DISAPPOINT.

PLEASE ADD 75P POSTAGE AND PACKING TO ALL ORDERS FOR STILLS AND AUDIO CASSETTES, £1.00 PER VIDEO. POSTERS A2 SIZE FREE P+P.

NAME .... ADDRESS ....
MEMBERSHIP NO. ....
DATE ORDERED ....

PLEASE SEND ORDERS TO:- J.C.F.C., MAIL ORDER, 15-17 FALCON RD, LONDON. SW11 2JP.

order for christmas

JACKIE CHAN FAN CLUB
presents

UK Premiere
POLICE STORY II
PLUS
DRAGONS FOREVER
PLUS
ARMOUR OF GOD
(All English versions)

SCALA CINEMA
275-277 PENTONVILLE RD KINGS CROSS LONDON
(NEXT TO BRITISH RAIL AND TUBE STATION)

SUNDAY JULY 23RD 1989 (DOORS OPEN 12.30PM)
(MERCHANDISE STALL SELLING VIDEOS, T-SHIRTS, POSTERS)

---- CUT HERE ----

TICKETS £6.00 (J.C.F.C. MEMBERS) £7.00 (NON-MEMBERS)
PLEASE SEND ME .... TICKETS
NAME ....
ADDRESS ....
MEMBERSHIP NO. .... TOTAL £ ....
SEND TO: J.C.F.C. TEMPO HOUSE 15-17 FALCON RD LONDON SW11 2PJ TEL. 223 4688

The U.K. JACKIE CHAN FAN CLUB

1989 will see the start of the first Official Jackie Chan Fan Club. Life time membership. Newsletters. Film news and reviews. Seminars. T-Shirts. Badges. Videos. Posters. Searchline. and much much more.

All interested in joining should write in the first instance to:

JACKIE CHAN FAN CLUB, P.O. BOX M.P.C. TEMPO HOUSE, FALCON RD, LONDON SW11 2PJ
01-223 7662. Ext. 206

JACKIE CHAN U.K. FAN CLUB

J.C.F.C.
incorporating
HEROES OF THE EAST
P.O. BOX
409
SE18 3DW.

Dear Mike.

I'm soughting out your videos. Sorry for delay. This is due to The Move. as way of an apology. Please find x2 Tickets for you to attend The film Show.

Thankyou for your Support

Rick

President: BEY LOGAN
Directors: RICKY BAKER,

ORDER FORM

PLEASE WRITE YOUR ORDER IN BLOCK CAPITALS IN THE SPACE PROVIDED BELOW:

T-SHIRTS:	POSTERS:
TOTAL £	TOTAL £

VIDEOS:
TOTAL £

OTHERS
TOTAL £

NAME ....
ADDRESS ....
TEL No .... AGE ....

SUB TOTAL: £
SUB TOTAL: £
SUB TOTAL: £
GRAND TOTAL: £
(enclosed)

PLEASE ALLOW 28 DAYS DELIVERY
SEND TO : J.C.F.C. P.O. 409 SE 18 3DW

J.C.F.C. IMPORTANT NOTICE

Dear Reader,

In our Newsletter No. 3, which was dispatched at the beginning of June, I would like to remind all our members that the response for the subscription to the bi-monthly newsletter is still very low. Some of you reading this will have already subscribed and I would personally like to thank you very much for keeping the faith. For those of you who have not, I would like to make one last plea for your support.

Since we opened in February, 1989 we believe we have done justice to Jackie Chan with the newsletters, the film shows (which if you have already attended, you will know just how brilliant they are) and a range of merchandise, and also in helping you improve your video collections, none of which would have happened if you had not shown your support.

Recently, whilst working with Jonathon Ross, he informed me that Jackie had spoken to him regarding his support in the U.K. and he believed that if he was not a success, it was because it was the way his movies go straight to video whereas in most other parts of the world his movies receive great theatrical premieres given the same respect and attention as Steven Spielberg would receive here.

We have tried to bring Jackie round by forming a UK chapter of the Fan Club knowing full well that should our fanship reach high numbers, Jackie would surely be forced to make an appearance in the U.K. Sadly, this will never be unless we all stick together.

The new Jackie Chan Newsletter will contain facts about Jackie, his early day movies, up to date facts, and more in depth film reviews, plus we want to start looking at other martial artists such as Samo Hung, Yuen Biao, Jean-Claude van Damme, Bradon Lee and some of the more traditional kung-fu movies.

I trust on reading this, you will do the right thing and subscribe; it can only benefit you. Tell your friends, bring them to the film shows and let them see what they are missing.

We would also like to bring our Roadshow to more areas around the U.K. for those less fortunate in travelling.

So, remember what I say, and keep the faith.

RICK BAKER.

JACKIE CHAN U.K. FAN CLUB

TEMPO HOUSE
15-17 Falcon Road, London S.W.11 2PJ.
Tel. 01-223-1688 Fax. 01-223-7116

Hi There Film Fan,

Thank you for your valuable order, in buying your videos directly from us help's us keep the J.C.F.C. alive.

We will be expanding on our video collection (inc. imports) and over the next 12 months, we will hope to have between 200-300 films on record, helping you to build a film library any enthusiast would be proud of.

Films will get regular reviews in our bi-monthly Newsletter available at £10.00 per 6 copies. Giving you an accurate guide on who's who in the martial arts/Hong Kong movie world, as we believe we are the No. 1 specialist in the U.K.

For any further information, please write to the J.C.F.C. enclosing a stamped addressed envelope.

Thank you for your continuing support.

Keep the faith.

Rick Baker   John Brennan

THANK YOU FOR JOINING THE JACKIE CHAN FAN CLUB. TO HELP IN OUR RESEARCH, WE HAVE LISTED BELOW OTHER FAMOUS MARTIAL ARTISTS WHO YOU MIGHT LIKE INFORMATION ON IN FUTURE MONTHLY NEWSLETTERS.

BRUCE LEE ☐   SAMO HUNG ☐   YUEN BIAO ☐   WANG JANG LEE ☐

SHO KOSUGI ☐   JEAN CLAUDE VAN DAMME ☐   CYNTHIA ROTHROCK ☐

MICHELLE KHAN ☐   GORDON LUI ☐   OTHERS ....

....

SUBSCRIPTION TO THE J.C.F.C. U.K. IS £10.00 (U.K. MEMBERS) £15.00 (OVERSEAS MEMBERS). THIS WILL ALSO INCLUDE A PACKAGE WHICH YOU WILL RECEIVE WITH YOUR FIRST NEWSLETTER. VIDEOS, POSTERS, T-SHIRTS, SWEATSHIRTS AND SEMINARS WILL BE AVAILABLE DURING 1989.

ALL CHEQUES/POSTAL ORDERS SHOULD BE MADE OUT TO THE JACKIE CHAN FAN CLUB.

ANYONE WITH ANY QUESTIONS ON JACKIE CHAN SHOULD WRITE TO THE ABOVE ADDRESS.

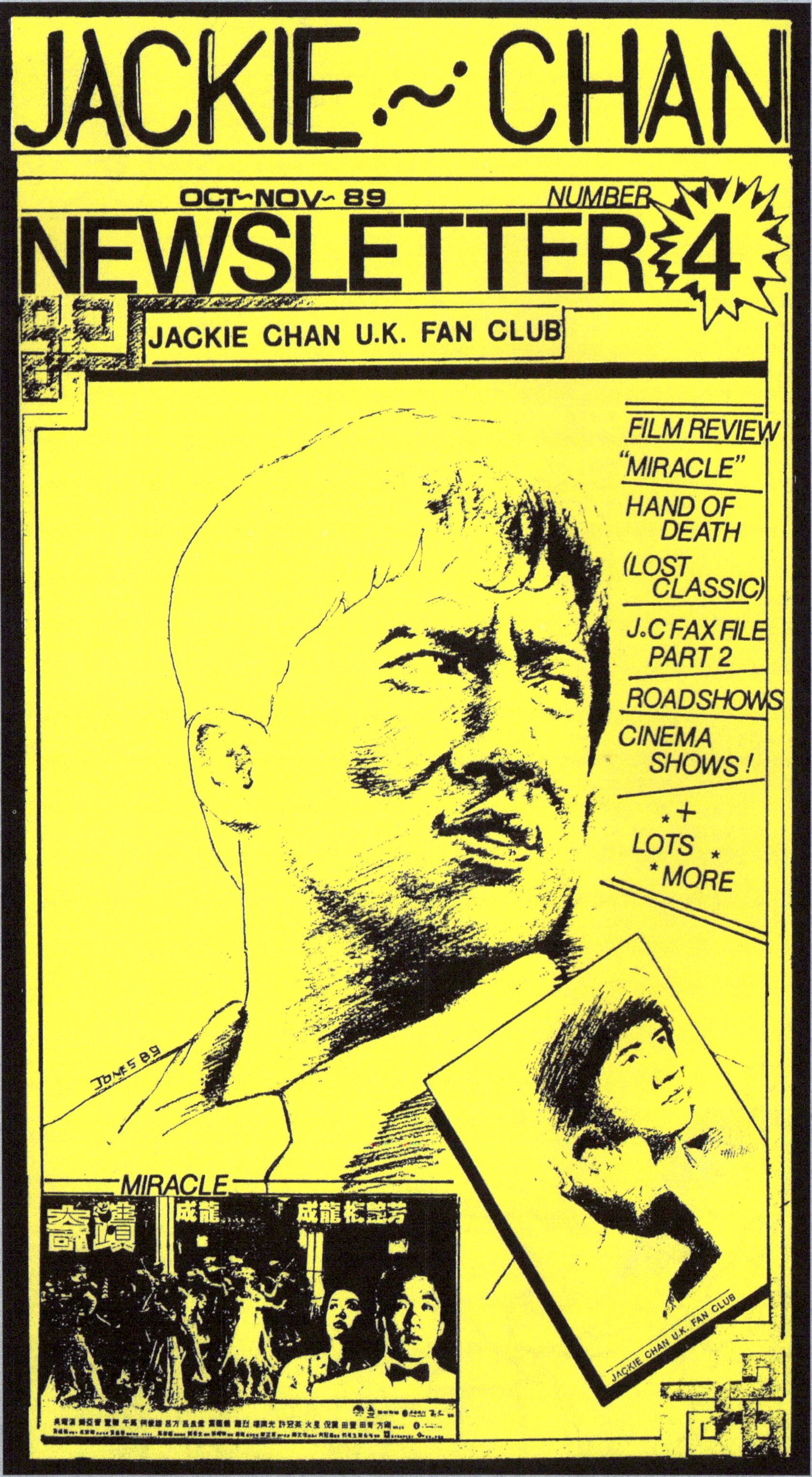

JACKIE ~ CHAN
NEWSLETTER OCT~NOV~89 NUMBER 4
JACKIE CHAN U.K. FAN CLUB

FILM REVIEW
"MIRACLE"
HAND OF DEATH
(LOST CLASSIC)
J.C FAX FILE PART 2
ROADSHOWS
CINEMA SHOWS!
+ LOTS MORE

MIRACLE

JACKIE CHAN U.K. FAN CLUB

TEMPO HOUSE, 15-17 FALCON ROAD, LONDON. SW11 2PJ
PHONE: 01-223-7662 EXT. 206   FAX: 01-223-7116

PRESIDENT BEY LOGAN . VICE PRESIDENT DEAN JONES

DIRECTORS RICKY BAKER & CHRIS ALEXIS

Hi there,

All you Jackie devotees and welcome to Newsletter Part II, the sequel.

Firstly, I would like to apologise for the delay with the first Newsletter; the main problem being that over the last few months we were inundated with letters from people enquiring about the J.C.F.C, and although the initial response was brilliant, it did not seem to produce that many paid subscribers. We had hoped to get a minimum of 300 paid members as a realistic starting point for the Fan Club, however, by February 1st we had only received 160 members. We thought that as soon as we moved into the J.C.F.C. offices, the applications would come flowing in, but by February 20th we were still 45 members short and we knew we could wait no longer. Thus the reason that the Newsletter was delayed. I am happy to say that since then, we have reached the 300 mark and, hopefully, now that the first newsletter has gone out, it will encourage more and more people to join, especially all those who enquired but have not sent their forms back (come on, let's get Jackie on the map!). So, tell all your friends, video shops, work mates, anybody who enjoys a few hours of class entertainment, to put pen to paper and join the J.C.F.C.

The Club is run independently by enthusiasts for enthusiasts, so if we all do our bit, 1989 will be the year that Jackie was put on the U.K. map.

Keep the faith.

Rick. *Ricky Baker*

JACKIE

POLICE STORY II
FULL REVIEW :- NEXT MONTH!

1995-1997 – The Jackie Chan USA Fan Club

The Jackie Chan USA Fan Club released its first newsletter in January 1995, and was not associated with the Official Fan Club that Willie Chan was running. Along with the membership card, you received a regular newsletter. The newsletter was reasonably good for an unofficial Fan Club, with a lot of up-to-date information on Jackie's current movies, and they even organized a trip to Hong Kong to meet Jackie in person. The Club was reasonably successful, but it couldn't compete with the Official Fan Club, especially with their newsletter being a black and white photocopy, and the officials being a colour magazine. The Fan Club ran for around three years, with the club folding shortly after starting up their own Web-site in February 1997, with officially announcing it in their May 1997 newsletter.

JACKIE CHAN USA FAN CLUB

ChanFansUS@aol.com
P. O. Box 2281
Portland, OR 97208
http:/www.spiritone.com/~chanfans
JULY 1997 Vol. 3, No. 7
Copyright 1997

"Our club's goal is to promote international friendship and understanding through a common interest."

—JACKIE CHAN 3/3/95

LATEST NEWS

Operation Condor will open on July 18 nationwide. A premiere is planned for **July 15 in New York** as well as an appearance on the David Letterman Show. Due to filming commitments in Rotterdam, Jackie plans to leave the USA the next day, meaning that there will be little or no opportunities to see him this trip.

For some reason, Miramax's Dimension Films thinks that Jackie plays a secret agent in this movie, which was originally *Armour of God, Part 2*. Seeing the ads, or poster, you might not think this was the same movie that was released in Cantonese several years ago. With creative editing, maybe it isn't !!

FAN CLUB ANNOUNCES FABULUOUS TOUR TO HONG KONG FOR SPECIAL JACKIE CHAN EXHIBITION!!! Mark your calendars for this once in a lifetime opportunity to be in Hong Kong when Jackie is there and to see and experience a unique and comprehensive exposition of Jackie Chan memorabilia, both from his personal collection and from his movies. Here's what's happening:

1) Free admission to the exhibition (which will feature Jackie's collection of stamps, cup and saucers, his trophies, props from his movies, photos through the years, and more!!);
2) Meet Jackie and autograph session at the exhibition;
3) Preview of Jackie's latest film, WHO AM I?;
4) Visit to Jackie's Hong Kong office;
5) Auction of Jackie's used clothing items and
6) A dinner party with Jackie (tentative).

Last January, Jackie's "dream came true" in Los Angeles, next January, the dream of every Jackie Chan fan can come true: To see Jackie in Hong Kong! There may never be another such golden and special opportunity as this. Why not? Because Jackie is so busy now, that getting him to make a commitment to be in Hong Kong, or anywhere for that matter, on any date far enough in advance for us to plan a tour is almost impossible. (Because most of his filming is done outside of Hong Kong, last year Jackie only spent about 2 weeks there altogether.) Because this exhibition is a unique event and will give the true Chan fan the opportunity to see all of the mementos and items that have meant so much to Jackie's career. And because, if you want to extend your stay for another day you can be there for Chinese New Year, January 28, the Year of the Tiger!!

Here are the travel details:
PRICE: $1190, includes:
Six nights in first class Hong Kong hotel from January 22, to January 28;
Round-trip air fare from Portland or Seattle;
Round-trip airport and hotel transfers in Hong Kong;
Half-day Hong Kong Island tour.
Optional: Visit other parts of China;
Trip cancellation insurance;
Additional stayover;
Plus other arrangements to meet your individual needs. I am working with a travel agent who will do his best to accommodate all your special needs. So if you are coming from somewhere else, don't worry, we can work out special arrangements. Planning to go to Taiwan, Korea, Japan, etc. at about that time? No problem, let us know, we'll work out a special itinerary.

Requirements:
Space is limited so reservations are on a first come first served basis. All who participate must be a **paid-up fan club member through January 1998**. A **$250 deposit** is required to reserve your place. (Please note that as this is still in the planning stages, there may some some charges for events in Hong Kong other than those listed above as being free or included.)

A Publication of the Jackie Chan Fan Club, USA
Joy C. Al-Sofi, President and Editor

1995-2001 – THE OFFICIAL JACKIE CHAN UK FAN CLUB

The Official Jackie Chan UK Fan Club was a division of the HK Jackie Chan Fan Club and was run by Richard Cooper and began around 1995, and became more active the following year. Along with the membership card, you originally received a regular newsletter. Richard also produced the Screen Power magazine dedicated to Jackie, but this was not really associated with the Fan Club itself. In March 1999 the newsletter became a fanzine, this only lasted four issues (March 2000), but from issue 5 onwards it went back to being a regular newsletter. The small fanzine was packed with quizzes, competitions, memorabilia, member's letters and up to date information on Jackie. Again like most Fan Clubs of the era, the birth of the internet made Fan Clubs obsolete, and Richard devoted more time on his Screen Power and Jade Screen magazines.

(I would like to thank Thorsten Boose for his help with some of the information I needed to complete this article. Look out for Thorsten's forthcoming Jackie Chan Fan Club publication).

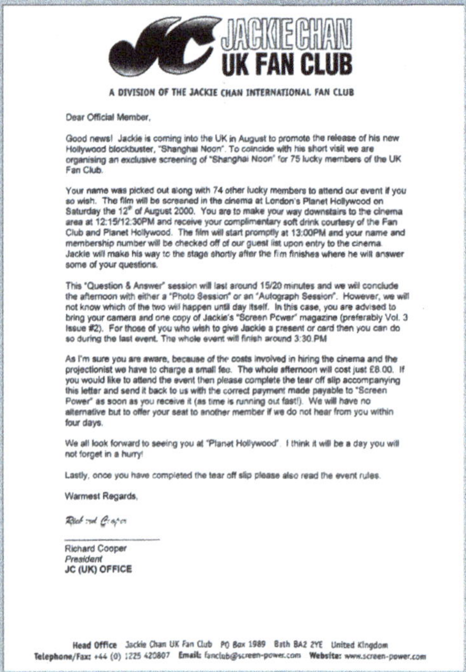
JACKIE CHAN
UK FAN CLUB

A DIVISION OF THE JACKIE CHAN INTERNATIONAL FAN CLUB

Dear Official Member,

Good news! Jackie is coming into the UK in August to promote the release of his new Hollywood blockbuster, "Shanghai Noon". To coincide with his short visit we are organising an exclusive screening of "Shanghai Noon" for 75 lucky members of the UK Fan Club.

Your name was picked out along with 74 other lucky members to attend our event if you so wish. The film will be screened in the cinema at London's Planet Hollywood on Saturday the 12th of August 2000. You are to make your way downstairs to the cinema area at 12:15/12:30PM and receive your complimentary soft drink courtesy of the Fan Club and Planet Hollywood. The film will start promptly at 13:00PM and your name and membership number will be checked off of our guest list upon entry to the cinema. Jackie will make his way to the stage shortly after the film finishes where he will answer some of your questions.

This "Question & Answer" session will last around 15/20 minutes and we will conclude the afternoon with either a "Photo Session" or an "Autograph Session". However, we will not know which of the two will happen until day itself. In this case, you are advised to bring your camera and one copy of Jackie's "Screen Power" magazine (preferably Vol. 3 Issue #2). For those of you who wish to give Jackie a present or card then you can do so during the last event. The whole event will finish around 3:30.PM

As I'm sure you are aware, because of the costs involved in hiring the cinema and the projectionist we have to charge a small fee. The whole afternoon will cost just £8.00. If you would like to attend the event then please complete the tear off slip accompanying this letter and send it back to us with the correct payment made payable to "Screen Power" as soon as you receive it (as time is running out fast!). We will have no alternative but to offer your seat to another member if we do not hear from you within four days.

We all look forward to seeing you at "Planet Hollywood". I think it will be a day you will not forget in a hurry!

Lastly, once you have completed the tear off slip please also read the event rules.

Warmest Regards,

Richard Cooper
President
JC (UK) OFFICE

Head Office Jackie Chan UK Fan Club PO Box 1989 Bath BA2 2YE United Kingdom
Telephone/Fax: +44 (0) 1225 420807 **Email:** fanclub@screen-power.com **Website:** www.screen-power.com

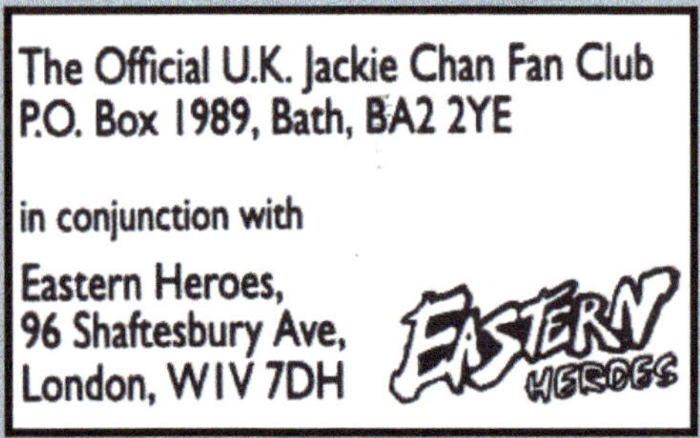

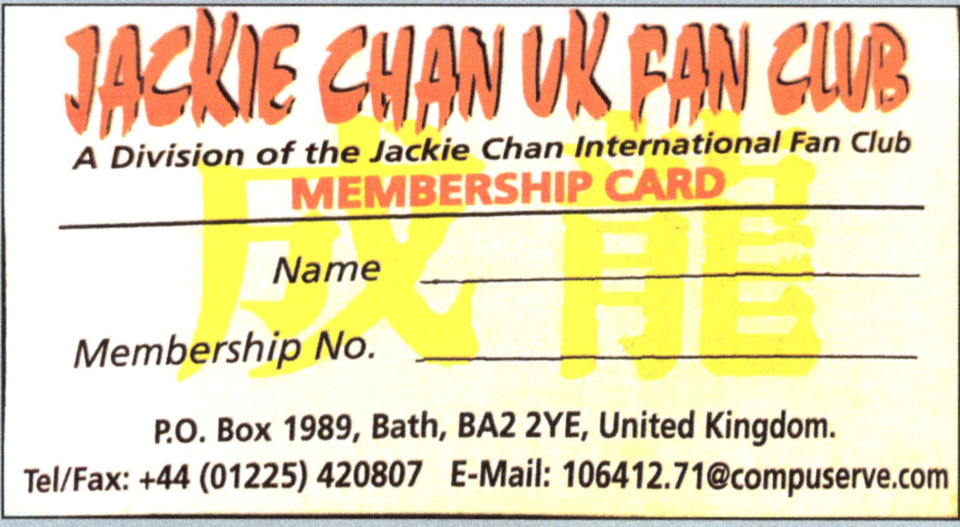

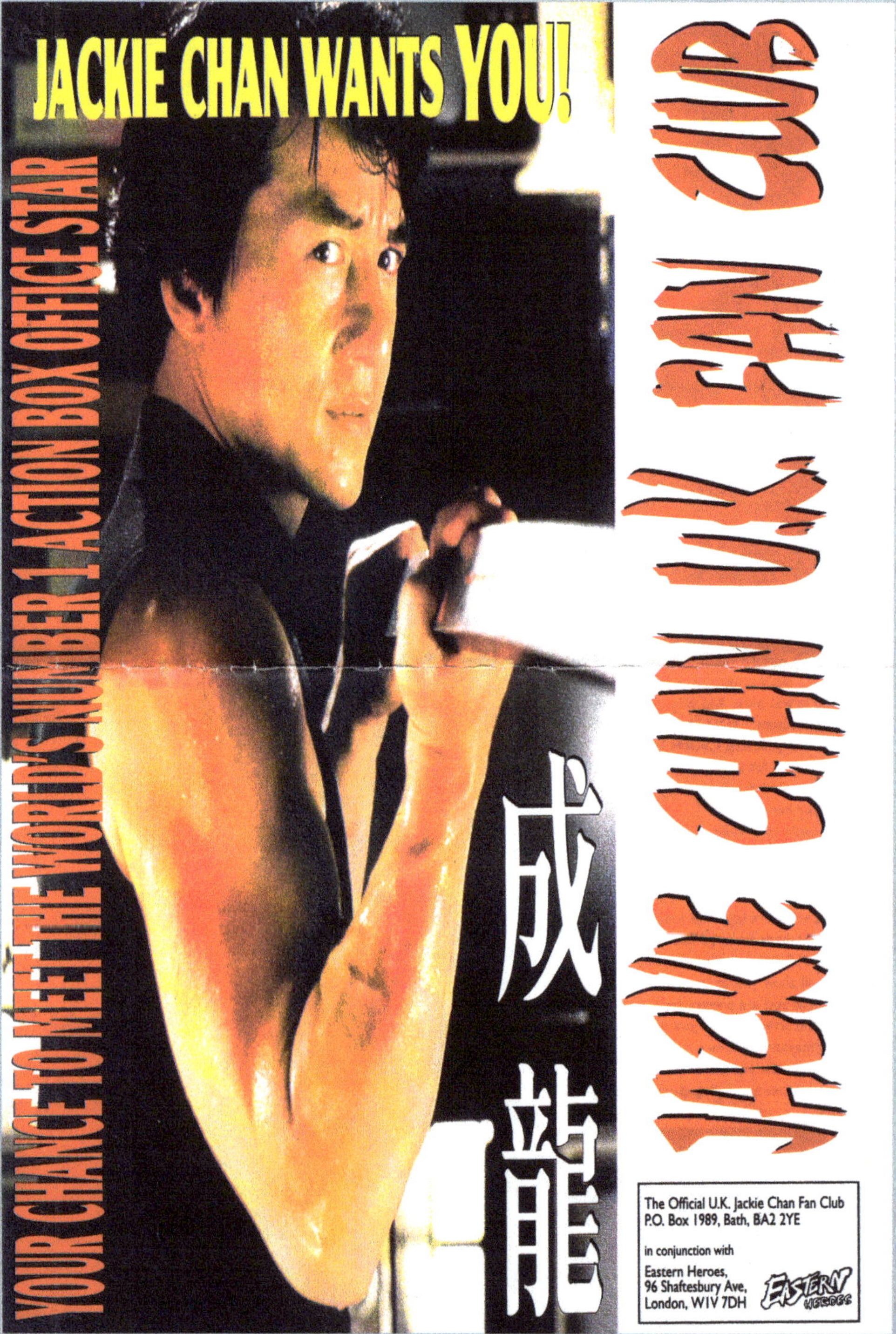

FAN ZONE

Welcome to a special edition of Eastern Heroes, dedicated to celebrating the life and legacy of one of cinema's most iconic figures: Jackie Chan. As we mark his 70th birthday, we are reminded of the profound impact he has had on countless lives around the globe.

For decades, Jackie Chan has captivated audiences with his awe-inspiring stunts, infectious charisma, and unmatched dedication to his craft. But beyond his on-screen prowess, Jackie has become a symbol of resilience, perseverance, and the power of following one's passion.

In this commemorative issue, we have gathered insights from a diverse array of Jackie Chan fans, each sharing their personal stories of how he has enriched their lives. From childhood memories of watching his films with wide-eyed wonder to adulthood admiration for his work ethic and humility, Jackie Chan's influence knows no bounds.

Many of our readers have graciously shared their stories and showcased their cherished memorabilia collections, showcasing everything from classic films to rare collectibles that serve as testaments to Jackie's enduring legacy. Through these artefacts, we are reminded of the countless hours of joy and inspiration that Jackie has brought into our lives.

As Jackie enters his seventh decade, his enthusiasm for entertaining audiences remains undiminished. His passion for pushing boundaries and defying expectations continues to inspire generations old and new.

We extend our heartfelt thanks to all those who contributed to this special issue, and we eagerly anticipate celebrating Jackie Chan's 75th birthday with even greater fervor. Join us as we pay tribute to a living legend, whose impact on the world of cinema and beyond will endure for generations to come.

Keeping the Faith

Rick Baker

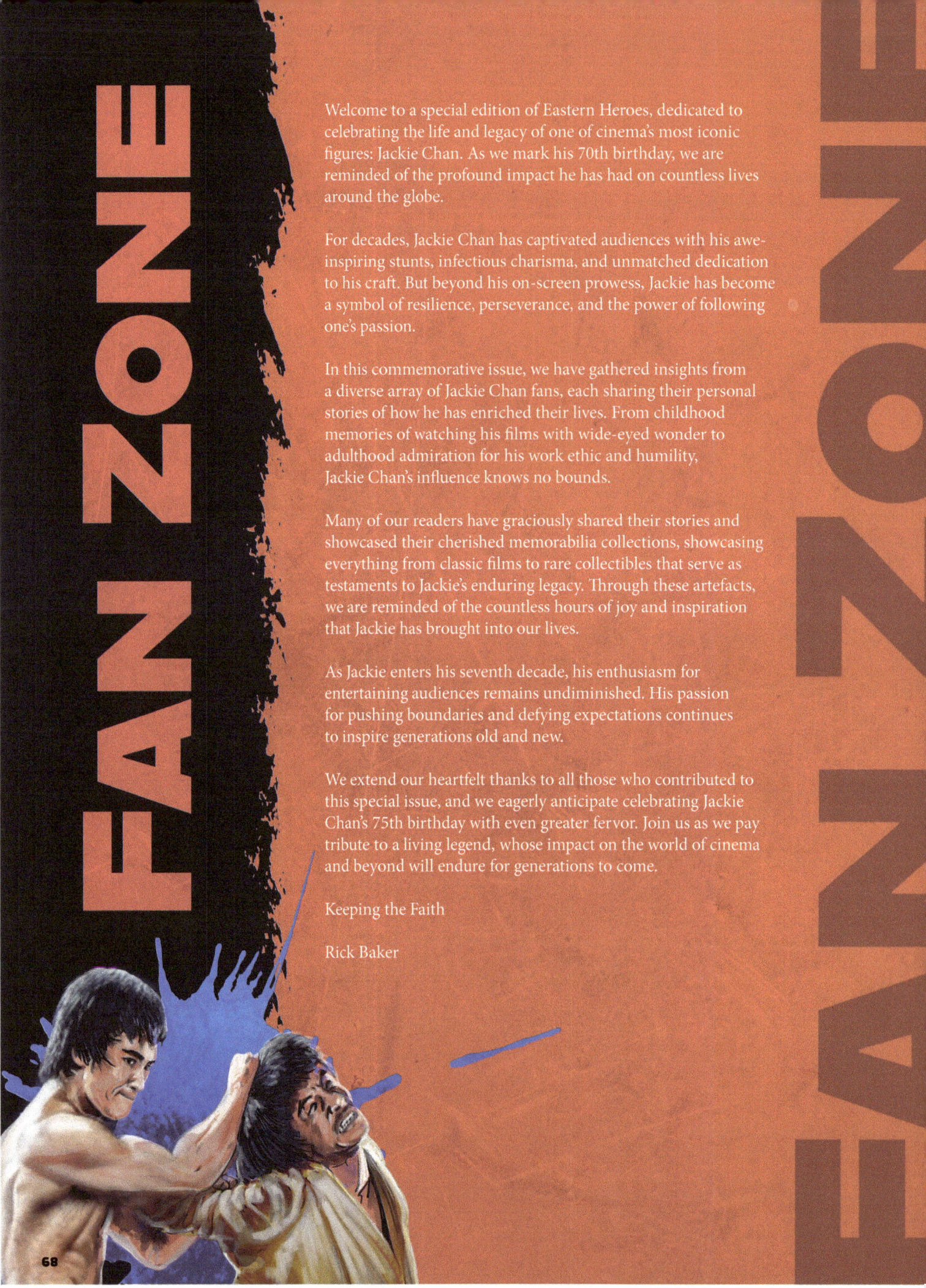

ANDY LONG NGUYEN

Andy Long (full name: Andreas Nguyen, Vietnamese) was born in 1988 and grew up in Germany. At a very young age Andy found his passion for martial arts movies due to the influence of world renowned movie star Jackie Chan. Inspired and fascinated by his idol, Andy tried hard to become as good and prolific as Jackie, training in different kinds of martial arts.

Time has passed so quickly. I still can't believe that Jackie turned 70 this year. It just feels like yesterday when Jackie celebrated his 60th birthday during our action prep of Dragon Blade. And it wasn't even too long ago when I've seen him for the first time on the set of *"Around the World in 80 Days"*, as a little fan waving behind the fence, when he wasn't even 50 yet.

Jackie Chan films have inspired and influenced my life as far back as I can remember.
As a young kid I could not think of anything else than working for him on one of his films.
I was an ordinary Vietnamese kid with a big dream, growing up in a small town in Germany where it seemed to be an impossible task to make this dream come true.
I always felt the pressure and feared that I wouldn't make it before he retires from action (not knowing that he would still make

movies until this date) So I have set myself a deadline of joining the stunt team whenever he would start to shoot his long announced third part of *Armour Of God aka Chinese Zodiac*.

In the meanwhile, I was still going to school and tried my best to prepare myself for the future by shooting my own fight scenes and short films with friends. The knowledge to do so came purely from studying Jackie's films on tape. Over the years I have edited a couple of Demo tapes with the footage I shot and tried to send it to Jackie but without any success.

When *Chinese Zodiac* was announced to start production and was promoted to be Jackie Chan's last action film, I knew that I have reached my deadline and that this would be my last chance to make my dream come true. I've manifested this goal and envisioned to work on this film to a point that I turned down any other upcoming job opportunities with the excuse that I'm going to work for Jackie Chan… without having any clue how, but I believed I will.

I was still young and knew nothing about this industry, who to approach and how to get on a movie. As a simple fan I reached out to every contact which seemed available to me and kept myself updated on Jackie Chan fan pages. Any little information was a blessing.

One day a picture was shared on the internet from one of the camera assistants of the crew stating that shooting with Big Brother in Paris has begun.

When I saw this picture, I had no more time to lose, and took my chance by traveling to Paris in hope that I'd find the set to reach Jackie and the stunt team.

I've hitchhiked to France with 50 euros in my pocket which I even had to borrow from my brother and tried to survive as long as I could on the streets of Paris until I would find the set of Chinese Zodiac but I had no idea where to start.

A week has passed, and it seemed so hopeless and ridiculous what I was doing but somehow I couldn't give up searching. Finally, only one of the many French stunt guys who I reached out to was kind enough to reply and was able to help me by sharing the location of the set. He even offered me to stay at his home for the next couple of days, which I'll never forget.

I managed to travel to the location, a huge park with a beautiful castle and luckily it was not completely blocked and still accessible for tourists. I've spotted the vans and trailers and

the entrance where the equipment was gathered and waited patiently in that area, until something would happen. I couldn't believe that I finally made it. When the crew was breaking for lunch, the stunt team came out of the castle and I tried to catch and speak to each of them and share my demo reels.

After everyone went to the catering, I took a moment to process what has happened and how lucky I was to finally be here, speaking to them. I was completely alone on the yard of the castle when suddenly Jackie appeared from far, passing by on his Segway on his way to lunch. I ran in front of him and had one copy of my demo reel left to hand it to him. It was only the two of us in the middle of the cord yard of the castle. He stopped and in this maybe 1 minute I had, I expressed my admiration and my wish of working for him, he kindly appreciated and took my demo reel, smiled and continued. It was unbelievable. My entire journey has led to this incredible moment.

The rest of the day I'd just enjoyed the privilege of being close to the set and tried to get a glimpse of the shoot as much as I could. Sometimes Jackie came out, he noticed me, smiled at me and went back in. When the day ended, I had to plan my next visit very carefully as I was already running out of my 50 Euros. In order to avoid the entrance fee, I had to break into the property of the castle. It was almost as adventures as the actual break-in-scene of the movie. The next days I'd show up on set again offering my help to move equipment whenever it was necessary. It was very surprising for everyone.

He Jun the Stunt Coordinator started to give me little tasks to help and support the team until even Jackie got used to see me every day and showed me how I could help out. He was extremely kind and always aware where I was standing, it seemed like he had eyes behind his back, even though I tried to be as invisible as possible he would suddenly turn around and speak to me as if he knew long back that I was standing behind him. He knew I was too shy to say something, so he always broke the silence and started the conversation to make me feel comfortable, but I was still too nervous to hold up the condensation for very long. When the shooting in Paris came to an end, I wasn't sure what is going to happen next, it felt like the end of the journey. But I knew that I have tried everything possible and went as far as I could to make them aware of my existence. I enjoyed every minute on the set and was the happiest that Jackie noticed me.

The entire time I was dying to take a picture with Jackie, but I held it back because I refused to believe that this would be the only chance I have. I was still holding on to the dream on officially working on this film. So, I went back without asking for a picture. A month later back in Germany I received an email by He Jun sharing that Jackie has seen my reel and both would like to give me the chance to work with them, if I'm ready to come to China. Immediately I went to process my visa and got ready.

I honestly didn't know what it meant, whether they just going to test me for a couple of days and send me back, but to my surprise I arrived in China and I was doing the same work as everyone else on the stunt team for the next 10 months, I was even chosen to perform the first stunt on screen. From there on everything went faster than I was able to process. The experience on this film was overwhelming and unforgettable. Jackie was always kind and fun and

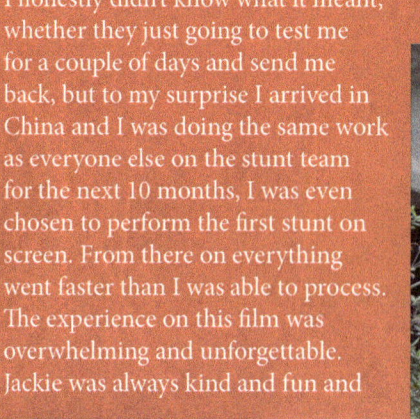

exactly the way I imagined him to be, an extremely passionate film maker, still doing incredible stunts at the age of 57, not sitting still for a minute and doing all kind of work on the set to bring the movie to life. He just loves the life on set and lives for making films as perfect as he can.

And when I thought that Jackie's last action movie came to an end, he promised that I shouldn't worry, it was just the beginning. Months later I've got the call for the next film and then next one… and the rest is history.

Today I'm blessed to work as an action director for the film industry and I try to apply everything I've learned from Jackie on every movie that I do.

Jackie has inspired me to step out of my comfort zone, dream big and make those dreams come true. I wish him to live a long, healthy and happy life, so that he can continue doing what he loves, making films and inspire many more generations the way he inspired me and so many others.

HAPPY 70th BIRTHDAY!!!

CARL TRAIL

Carl Reflects on his lifelong passion for Jackie Chan, and let us have a sneak peek at his long life passion collecting JC Movies and memorabilia.

Hi, my name is Carl and I have been a fan of Jackie ever since I was 2 years old when my parents rented Police Story from a local video shop way back in the mid 80's. I've collected his movies on countless videos, DVD's and in recent years Blu-Ray's along with soundtracks, posters, and books etc. Anything to do with Jackie Chan I'd get but the best day of my life was when I finally met my idol back in 2000 when I was 16 at the UK premier of Shanghai Noon in Leicester Square.

I had not long joined the JC UK Fan Club and I received a letter on Wednesday 9th August saying Jackie was coming to the UK for the Premier of Shanghai Noon and the UK Fan Club have been invited to attend, and after the movie the UK Fan Club where invited across the street to meet Jackie at Planet Hollywood and the letter said to make sure we have a polaroid camera if we want a photo with Jackie. The Premier was to be held on Saturday the 12th August so my Mum had to rush to get things sorted, buy a polaroid, return the RSVP, buy the train tickets etc. Also I wanted to give Jackie a present so I got him a cup and saucer because I knew that's what he liked to collect.

On the Saturday morning my Mum woke me up at 4 am by saying "Come on Carl,

we're going to meet Jackie Chan". It felt like Christmas had come early!

We had to get the train at 5 in the morning, we live in the North West of England and would be in London by 10 AM. When we got to Euston Station my Mum was worrying about how to get to Leicester Square because it was our first time in London and I ended up saying "Euston we have a problem!". My Mum nearly dropped to the floor because she was laughing so hard. We found the London Underground and somehow we managed to find where we needed to go. When we got to the Odeon cinema there were people waiting behind barriers but since we had tickets we walked straight in. We got to our seats and there were free issues of Screen Power on the seats. My mum wanted some popcorn so I went to get some and when I went back to Screen One, I walked through the doors and there was some steps to walk up and at the top there was a gentleman standing at the top so I politely said excuse me and thank you as I passed. I didn't look at the man because I was keeping an eye on everything I just bought and didn't want to drop them. When I got to my seat I looked back and saw it was Willie Chan. About 30 seconds later Jackie walked in and jogged to the front of the screen while waving to everyone. Obviously I knew I was meeting him after the movie but just seeing him there in person I was in absolute awe. Jackie thanked everyone for coming and hoped we'll like the movie and did we.

After the movie we rushed over to Planet Hollywood and had to queue at the top of a spiral staircase. We were second in line behind a lovely lady we started talking to who had brought along the first issue of Screen Power and when we where told to go down, me and the lady pushed my Mum to the front. We got so nervous, you'd think we where going into Pasaje del Terror in Blackpool!

We were lead into a small screening room and I thought we were going to watch something else to do with Jackie before he came out. when it filled up Jackie came out after a few minutes waiting and he walked to the little stage at the front and just like before we saw Shanghai Noon I was in disbelief that I was in the same room as my all time favourite actor.

He asked if we all enjoyed the movie. He just flew in from Istanbul and that he'd just done a big stunt for his next movie (Accidental Spy). He also said he would like to set Shanghai Noon 2 in London and that he already has an idea for a fight scene with an

umbrella like Gene Kelly. It came to fruition three years later in Shanghai Knights.

After saying thanks for all our support Richard Cooper told us to line up for a photo with Jackie and me and my Mum was 2nd in line again. When it was our turn Jackie asked how are we and I couldn't speak but my Mum said "we're fine thanks" and she told him how much of a fan I've been ever since I was a baby. He stood between us and we put our arms around him for a picture and his assistant took it with our polaroid and then she took another with another camera and then we were rushed off the stage but my Mum turned to Richard Cooper and said "hang on my son has a present for Jackie" so I went back and handed Jackie the gift bag and he continuously bowed and said thank you and I continuously bowed and said you're welcome as I slowly walked backwards towards the exit.

When we left we went to an American diner for something to eat and you can tell it was full of Jackie Chan fans because they where all reading the Screen Power magazine.

After a little look around we headed home. A year later I needed an operation and my Mum wrote to Jackie about my situation and asked for an autograph and 6 weeks later I got a letter from Willie Chan and a signed photo of jackie saying "Dear Carl, Have faith, be strong and our dreams can come true! Love Jackie".

It has been 24 years since I met Jackie but I still dream and hope I can meet him again some day and hopefully I would be less shy and will be able to talk to him more but most of all say thank you.

**CHRISTOPHER DALY
[TIGER BLADE]**

Having an avid interest in Martial Arts and training since 1979, it was around 1981, when I was first exposed to Jackie Chan. As he exploded onto our family TV set in movies like Shaolin *Wooden Men*, *Drunken Master* and *Snake In The Eagles Shadow*, I was then instantly hooked on this Incredible star, Jackie Chan. This man inspired me to do more in my own training, become more explosive, graceful and animate. I could not wait until the Video Rental store stocked up on new releases, I followed every movie

I could possibly get hold of. For me the stunt work and martial action choreography played a huge role in my own training, eventually creating demonstrations for my club and tournaments. I absolutely adored everything in these movies like *Wheels on Meals* (my own personal favourite), *Winners and Sinners*, *My Lucky Stars*. The combination of music, sound score, action, fashion and of course JACKIE CHAN, I was so taken by everything, I even wore clothes to emulate his, right down to the Diadora footwear. Moving into the 1990s, I became a movie reviewer for two magazines, 'Martial Arts Illustrated' and 'Impact The Action Movie Magazine', and I was totally stoked to review Jackie Chan Movies such as *Twin Dragons* and *City Hunter*, it was all like

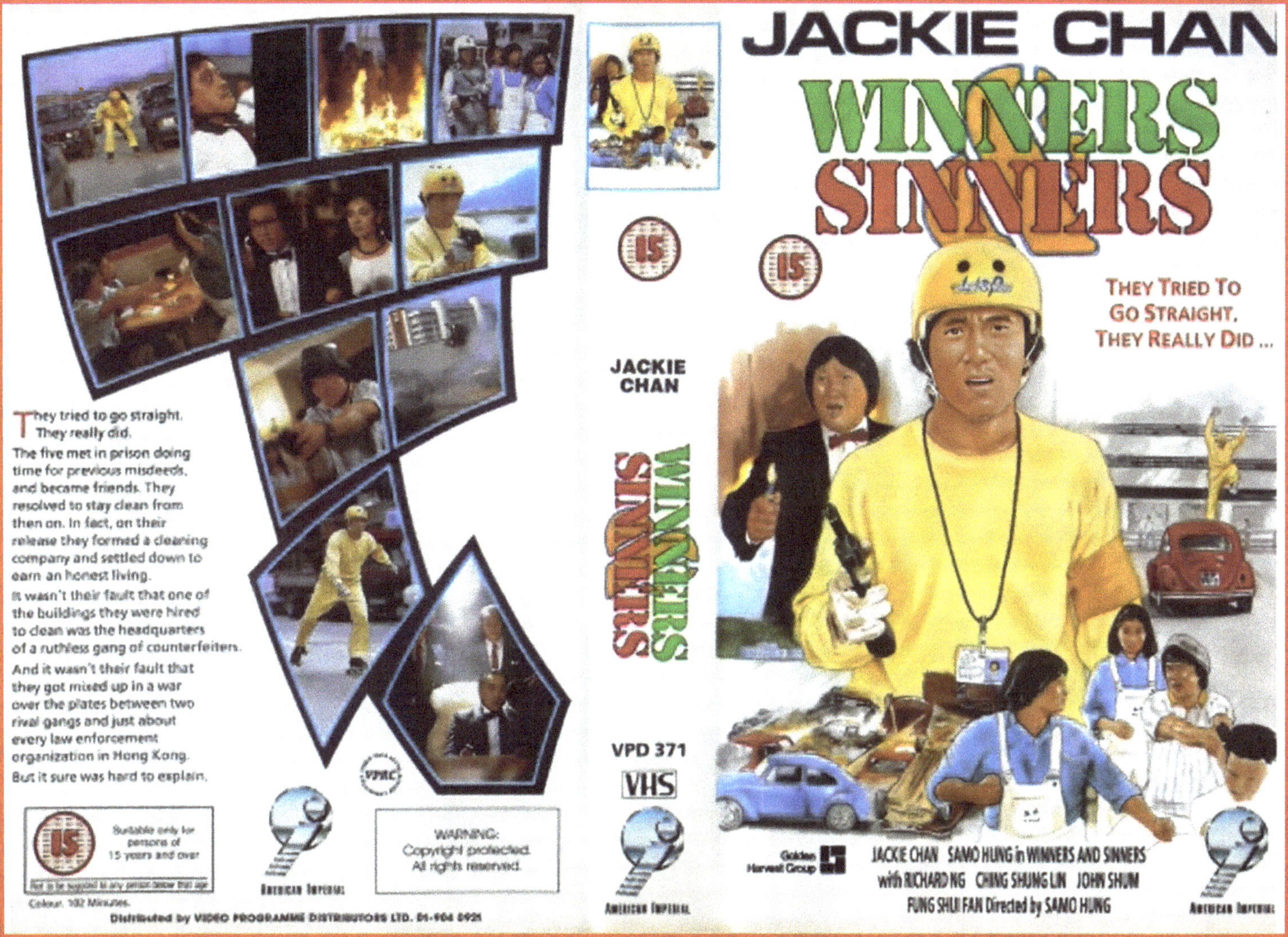
They tried to go straight.
They really did.
The five met in prison doing time for previous misdeeds, and became friends. They resolved to stay clean from then on. In fact, on their release they formed a cleaning company and settled down to earn an honest living.
It wasn't their fault that one of the buildings they were hired to clean was the headquarters of a ruthless gang of counterfeiters.
And it wasn't their fault that they got mixed up in a war over the plates between two rival gangs and just about every law enforcement organization in Hong Kong.
But it sure was hard to explain.
15
Suitable only for persons of 15 years and over
Not to be supplied to any person below that age
Colour. 102 Minutes.
WARNING: Copyright protected. All rights reserved.
Distributed by VIDEO PROGRAMME DISTRIBUTORS LTD.
JACKIE CHAN
WINNERS SINNERS
VPD 371
VHS
JACKIE CHAN
WINNERS SINNERS
THEY TRIED TO GO STRAIGHT. THEY REALLY DID ...
Golden Harvest Group
JACKIE CHAN SAMO HUNG in WINNERS AND SINNERS
with RICHARD NG CHING SHUNG LIN JOHN SHUM
FUNG SHUI FAN Directed by SAMO HUNG

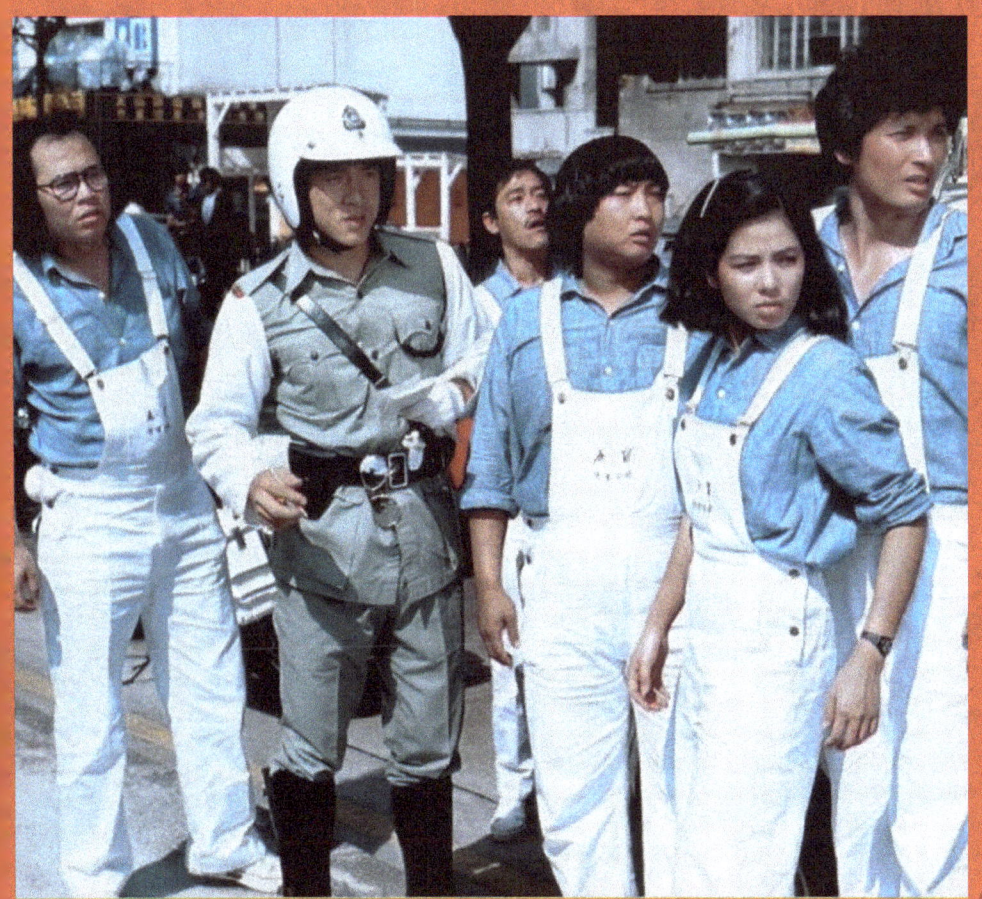

some kind of crescendo to reaching my own goal of travelling to Hong Kong to become a stuntman there, which unfortunately never materialized for me, however, the passion remained and I have always been a great fan of the incredible Jackie Chan. His embodiment of a never give up attitude and taking any opportunity that may arise regardless of risk, is always prevalent, and is something that he has instilled within me, pushing myself striving for absolute excellence, I think such an attitude and behaviour makes for a better individual.

The combination of Jackie Chan's kindness, determination and integrity, I believe are all handed down to many of those among his company, his stunt team (Sin Ga Ban) and to those he meets, and also to those that he hasn't met who admire Jackie Chan the way I do. The reach he has made out to people is purely magnificent to the point in his own words he didn't know how half the people who knew about him knew about him. Such a humble, friendly manner he has, and I believe that's just one thing everyone loves about, JACKIE CHAN.

DAVID GALLAGHER

It's 1993. I'm 8 years old. I've just seen the best film ever made with the coolest new guy on Earth starring in it. The masterpiece in question is *Twin Dragons* and the dude with attitude (hey, it's 1993…we spoke like that) is Jackie Chan.

It's 2023. I'm 38 years old. I've just watched a kind of average comedy with an icon of cinema I feel like I know personally in it. The average comedy in question is "*Twin Dragons*" Again, the icon that's like an old friend? Well, still Jackie. We're on first name terms now.

Jackie is turning 70 the day I write this. Others will have their takes on personal memories, memorabilia and the likes. I would like, with your permission to pay my tribute by focusing on one aspect that is the most important to me - his works. Especially on how to see the films in 2024 and why there's never been a better time to purchase Jackie on home video.

When I watched *Twin Dragons* as a boy I'd not seen movement like Jackie with limbs flying faster and with more fluidity than those steroid poseurs Arnie and Sly could dream of. He moved with pace and precision the hulking brutish Hollywood alternatives were too stiff to even consider. Jackie was NEW. The American stars were relics of the 80s. And the titular dragons of the title meant, there were two of him on screen at the same time - identical twins - twice the action! By the time I revisited the film for the-then new Blu-ray I'd seen just about every frame of Jackie's career that was available. I don't think anyone reading this tome would need told that *Twin Dragons* was a somewhat minor release for

him released at a crossroads of his career where he was trying to cross over to a more international audience (read: America) with a clean-cut image. My 8 year old self would be shocked that Jackie hadn't been that new in 1993 after all. Turns out he'd been making films for decades at that point. The effects, of having the twins on screen together, and at the same time, didn't hold up and that's being kind. My 1993 self would not have appreciated why the rest of this article was important - to celebrate Jackie's work, to ensure it remains in the best quality for posterity and to have copies of the films that explore and educate on the movies with as much passion and quality as "serious" filmmakers like Ozu, Mizoguchi, Wong Kar Wai and Kurosawa receive. Jackie gets that level of appreciation now. He's not stuffed into the corner of a video shop or late night on Channel 4 as a novelty from Hong Kong to watch do crazy stunts. He's finally accepted widely as an artist and auteur and his work is presented as such.

Despite *Twin Dragons* not quite remaining a classic anywhere but in the memory of an 8 year old it received a stunning new Blu-ray from 88 Films presented in a hard rigid collector's box with newly commissioned painted artwork. It had a double sided poster, art-cards and a thorough 80 page book on the film's production and place in Jackie's career. There was a commentary from Asian film experts Frank Djeng and F.J. DeSanto dissecting the film frame-by-frame. There was even an alternate version of the film, butchered - as many of Jackie's works were - by U.S. distributors who thought they could re-edit his earlier works and have a hit leeching off the success of *Rumble In The Bronx* in 1996. Archival interviews with Jackie, new interviews with supporting actors Tung Wei and James Ha, press kits, deleted scenes, trailers and a host of audio options from Cantonese mono or stereo, an English dub with new subtitles. This was a seriously in depth, celebratory release, surely? Was *Twin Dragons* a classic after all, to receive this treatment? Well...no.

In an age where physical media sales have slumped to an all-time low, one area thrives. They are the boutique film labels, "Criterion, Eureka, Arrow, Radiance", and seemingly a million more. They rely on a smaller audience but a devoted one. To get sales they put together packages like the aforementioned *Twin Dragons* from 88 Films. The VHS I rented 31 years ago was like any other - a cut down of the poster slapped on the cover, a blurb on the bag, some out of focus screen shots and Bob's your uncle. That wouldn't wash now. We live in a golden age of cult and art-house film receiving this sort of treatment. Jackie Chan, now 70 years old, is more than well served by the modern boutiques.

Jackie has been working in film for almost all of his 70 years debuting with his lifelong friend and collaborator Sammo Hung in 1962's Big and Little Wong Tin Bar. In his storied career most of his Hong Kong work has been with Lo Wei productions when Wei was trying to sell Jackie as the new Bruce Lee only for their relationship to sour (an understatement - Wei involved Triads to try and convince Jackie to stay on with him) and Jackie began a long, fruitful relationship with the legendary Golden Harvest. When he did finally crack the American market he had his films released by many distributors from Touchstone to Tri-Star and Disney to DreamWorks.

The films for which we, the faithful, idolise Jackie for most have been spectacularly well served in this era of boutique home media. It only makes sense. Jackie is a superstar but conversely also a cult hero. His fans want the best editions possible and the sort of extras package described above. He inspires intrigue. We want to know the stories behind the scenes. Jackie knows this - hence his famous outtakes reels over end credits. We want to peek behind the curtains. 88 Films have served Jackie's fans remarkably well. We have had superlative editions of the Lo Wei era films. His less popular (among traditional fans) American films have even received a level of care with The Medallion being released late last year.

The labels know Jackie has us - a fan base who will support his works being released even when they aren't our favourites. We are completest. We're seeing the first 4Ks now with the likes of Dragons Forever showing the highest quality picture of any Chan film on home video. Lest this become an advert for 88 Films, Eureka have also released some sublime editions. Their box set on 4K with the Police Story films combines an embarrassment of riches with the films looking remarkable. Editions of the Lucky

Stars films, Project A, Drunken Master and Meals On Wheels are also no doubt on shelves of many reading this. Booklets don't just focus on the same topics as the disc extras but feature treasure like explorations of Jackie's music career, his video game history, relationship with advertisers and many more with pictures that we have either not seen in the west or have only on black and white fanzine copies. It is no exaggeration to say that you could become a true Jackie scholar just from studying the boutique extra features. America has always been late to the party with Jackie but even they have finally started to release some wonderful editions there - Criterion and Shout Factory both having box sets of his work that features a lot of the titles released in the UK already.

As this goes to press we are about to see deluxe releases of Island Of Fire and Fearless Hyena 2 in the UK. These are, fair to say, favourites for a of few of us. Yet they receive the same love and care as the canonical classics. A true gift, even the titles owned by major studios have been opened up in recent years - Warner Archive/HMV in the UK has released Mr Nice Guy and the essential Drunken Master II.

So perhaps you are someone who has some reasonable DVDs and thinks that you don't need to buy them all again. Frankly, the upgrades, in picture quality and the content of the extras, makes this a no-brainer. If you have the inclination to buy a book like this, you will want a healthy dose of the titles released from the labels above.

Of course a lot of his more modern films are also available easily on standard blurays. 21st century films where Jackie has shown he's, as he likes to say "an actor who does stunts, not a stuntman who acts" like The Shinjuku Incident, Shaolin, Little Big Soldier, New Police Story, Police Story 2013 and The Foreigner featuring some of his greatest performances where he shows - as we fans knew - that Jackie is right in his words -he is so much more than stunts and action. Yet the discs they are on are either barebones or with inconsequential press kit extras. One can hope that one day they receive the same love as his earlier works have. Perhaps we will even learn to love Kung Fu Yoga and Vanguard. Though the latter DOES have Jackie singing Adele's Rolling In The Deep so, that needs an hour long documentary alone!

I can think of no better tribute to Jackie's status as an elder statesman of film than to talk about this side of his work - the side we can own and cherish. We can chart in depth the life, times and career of a man who has risen from the kid Bruce Lee took a shine to on the Enter The Dragon shoot to become every bit as well known as Lee himself. Yet Jackie has had the time Lee's death robbed him of to show his diverse talents as an actor, choreographer, director and more. You owe it to yourself to make sure you have the best presentations of his life's work - the films. The reason he started, the reason he became a superstar and the reason he is immortal.

We love you Jackie. We want to see you on sets in 30 years telling the young 'uns how to do it as you hit a century old.

About: Davy Gallagher is a film obsessive who runs a Youtube channel - Davy's Flicks (@davysflicks) - where he can be seen discussing what he has here - the history of film via physical media.

GARETH SMITH

Gareth recounts his love for Jackie and showcases some of the memorabilia he has acquired over the years

Hi, I'm Gareth Smith, 37, from Leeds, England, and I'm a Jackie Chan fan. I've been a fan of Jackie since I was a kid, around 3 or maybe 4 years old.

My first Jackie Chan film I watched was "*The Big Brawl*" on VHS. It was our kid's tape (the video collection label) with no box or cover. I vividly remember the opening credits and its song. I always had it on replay in my house. My dad would end up renting "*Police Story 3*" for me from my local shop, and although I never remembered the film, I never forgot its end sequence of him dangling from the helicopter ladder. Then, a couple of years later, a friend who lived down the street invited me and other friends to watch this amazing film he got. The way he described it, we had to watch it. It ended up being "*Rumble in the Bronx*," a bootleg tape of the Miramax cut. Not seeing Jackie for a couple of years, I recognized him, saying to my mates, "He's amazing!" Then we witnessed an amazing film, blown away by his stunts and the fight choreography. We were amazed at what we saw.

After this film, it's 1997, so I'm 10, and I regularly visit Castleford on a Saturday with my mum and dad. There was a particular video stall, and as I'm looking, my eyes were drawn to a particular tape. It would be "*Police Story: The Gold*," a front tape, and my mum insisted on buying it, as she was a fan too and instrumental in my movie taste growing up. She enjoys his films, and she bought it for me. Once home, I put it into the player while having a McDonalds. What I witnessed over the 90 minutes truly and utterly blew me away. My mind was blown at what I saw: the stunts, fights, comedy, and its dubbing; everything was a masterpiece. I had to tell my mates about this film the next day. They wouldn't believe what I told them until we watched the film together.

This film would then make me try to hunt every film he made. I had no Internet at the time, no PC. The fun of visiting any video shop, car boot, or market stall anywhere I went. I was lucky my mum was an action movie fan; she would buy the tapes, and we would watch them together. She's the reason why I'm a Jackie Chan fan.

My collection grew, then dwindled when we moved away and downsized, and my VHS tapes were sacrificed in the move. But over the years, my DVD collection grew, and now adding these beautifully made bespoke deluxe editions we're getting. Now, in my 30s, I've collected all my VHS back and ones

I was never able to get as a kid. It's been fun eBay stalking and joining private groups.

Jackie Chan, to me, is the greatest action star in the world. His bravery to do the stunts he's done for our entertainment is amazing, and his style of kung fu comedy is trendsetting. In his older years, he's showing great acting chops. Long live the legendary Jackie Chan.

HARRIET CONNOR

Fatty-Karate's Fantastic Collection!
By Harriet Conner.
Why I love "*First Mission*" Aka "*Heart of The Dragon*" starring Sammo Hung & Jackie Chan.

So, you're probably all wondering what I have been up to since you last heard from me all the way back in 2022. I've finally got my first kyu belt (after the pandemic putting my training on hold for a year and a half). I met Cynthia Rothrock (TWICE, might I add, thanks to various friends of mine and some very understanding convention staff), and I somehow managed to acquire more copies of "*Heart of Dragon.*"

When I wrote my article about how Sammo Hung inspired me to take up karate for Eastern Heroes' Sammo Hung special back in 2022, I only had five copies. Since I wrote that piece, I have somehow managed to acquire thirteen more copies, bringing my collection up to a whopping eighteen copies of what I consider to be one of Sammo Hung's greatest movies.

A number of people got in contact with me via social media and asked, "Fatty-Karate, why that movie in particular? Why not a more interesting Sammo movie, something like "*Eastern Condors*" or, "*Millionaire's Express*"?" To me, that movie is interesting. It sums up what being an autistic person is like (to the point I would recommend watching this back-to-back with Rain Man). Sammo's character definitely reminded me of myself and some other autistic adults I have known in my life. It has a good beginning, middle, and end, and whilst Jackie's character is not particularly pleasant towards Sammo, he does redeem himself at the end (although the same cannot be said

of some of the other characters, such as the cafe owner played by Wu Ma; however, they are usually only in the movie for one scene and are just there to advance the plot and to show Sammo and Jackie's day-to-day life). However, a couple of people have also contacted me to ask how I managed to collect so many copies, so I guess that's what this is - a rundown of how I came across all of my copies of "*Heart of Dragon.*" The first copy I ever purchased was the Hong Kong Legends DVD back in 2019. I had initially intended for that to be my only copy because obviously I wanted to save on space and money. I had genuinely not intended for my collection to balloon the way it did over the last 4 years of collecting. Yet when 88 Films announced their Blu-

ray release of the film during lockdown in 2020, I knew I had to have it - partly because I thought the cover art was amazing but also partly because I love that movie. "Two copies and that's enough," I thought to myself when I pre-ordered the Blu-ray on Amazon. "There are so many other movies out there I want to buy. I don't need more than two copies." Of course, I didn't stick to that. I decided I needed more copies of this movie and soon went hunting on eBay for more additions to my collection.

2021 (the second year of lockdown) saw the arrival of another Blu-ray, a VCD, a DVD, and 2 VHS tapes into my collection. The VHS tapes were bought primarily because I thought the covers were interesting, but also so I could have my favorite Sammo movie on a format that I have not willingly collected since childhood (I do eventually plan on buying a VHS player - I mean, VHS is making a comeback so I reckon it shouldn't be too hard for me to find one for a decent price). The VCD, which arrived with a slightly damaged case, was bought to see if VCD quality was really as bad as some of my friends said it was ("It's like watching a film made of LEGO bricks" is how a Hong Kong friend put it to me when I informed him of my purchase). Whilst VCD quality is not that great, it is by no means unwatchable - the video and audio qualities are just outdated in comparison to more modern formats like Blu-ray.
The Blu-ray I added to my collection in 2021 was a copy from Hong Kong, which was bought purely because I wanted a copy from Hong Kong (and also again because I liked the cover - I genuinely thought it was quite sweet), and the DVD was the one that was released as part of the Jackie Chan box set that was released by Hong Kong Legends that I picked up in CEX (I bought the box set as I didn't have a DVD copy of Crime Story at the time and figured I may never see another one out in the wild again as my local CEX very rarely gets any decent international cinema DVDs in. Most of the world cinema stock people trade in at my local branch tends to be anime).
In 2022, I added two DVD copies to my collection at the beginning of the year (the American release by 20th Century Fox with the red cover and a Hong Kong release with a lovely sky blue cover). That year also saw the addition of my first-ever laserdisc to my collection of Asian cinema, and probably the only laserdisc I am ever going to own. A friend of mine on Twitter messaged me saying they were having a clear out and had found something in their loft they thought I might like, and could they maybe send it to me. I agreed to let them send me the mystery item, guessing that it would most likely be a Sammo movie, and if not, then definitely something Hong Kong cinema related. A few days later, when a thin, square package arrived at my house, I wondered what exactly it was, thinking it may either be a laserdisc or a vinyl record. Upon opening the package, I was surprised yet happy to see a laserdisc of "Heart of Dragon." Sadly, I do not have a laserdisc player, so I cannot see if it works or not, but it is a lovely item to have.
I also added my first European copy to my collection in 2022 - a French language DVD that I picked up on eBay after being unable to find a copy whilst on holiday in France (I instead bought *Millionaire's Express*, which was the only Sammo one I could find in the branch of FNAC I visited). Another VCD soon followed this time one from the Philippines.

My collection nearly doubled in size in 2023. Arrow Films announced they were releasing the film on Blu-ray in the USA with all new cover art. "It's the same film you have many other copies of, just with new cover art," I told myself, trying my hardest to resist buying it. After all, I already had 2 other Blu-ray copies of the movie - why would I need another one? It would just take up space, after all space that could be used to store other movies. Of course, me being me, I bought it. I went for the classic *First Mission* slipcase, which has the all-new artwork on the Blu-ray case itself. Another couple of DVD copies soon followed (a Powerman III one from Germany and an Il Prima Missione one from Italy) thanks to endless hours spent scouring eBay and Amazon for copies I did not yet have, followed by 2 more VHS tapes and yet another VCD.

If I had to choose what my favorite copy I own would be, I would say probably the Hong Kong Blu-ray purely for the cover art alone. The cover art for most other releases doesn't really give you an idea of what the film is about - most releases feature Jackie on his

HING HL

I began my training in martial arts in 1983. My biggest influence was, of course, Bruce Lee, and the first movie I ever got my dad to rent out was "*Way of the Dragon.*" But, you know, around the same time, I became aware of a couple of new movies, namely "*The Young Master*" and the other one being "*Dragon Lord.*" I remember getting so excited renting these videos from my local video shop. It really didn't matter to me that they weren't in the original language. I had a new and different kind of gung fu hero, and his name was Jackie Chan.

My video player came alive when Jackie Chan was on the screen. His screen presence was awesome, and his stunts were thrilling. Jackie vs. Wong In-Shik is absolutely unforgettable. To this day, I find that lock flow incredible to watch, and I don't believe it's been imitated in any other martial arts film (otherwise I'd remember it, right?) Jackie's comedic reaction after he finally escapes the villain's grip is timeless. He mixed his martial arts theatrical prowess with a healthy injection of humour. In those early days, Jackie would be the unassuming underdog, the guy you would always want to win and cheer for. And then in 1984, "*Project A*" came along. My brother and I would always pose the way Sammo and Jackie did karate style in that restaurant fight. We'd have a lot of fun. And that's what our heroes do; give us fun memories that last a lifetime. I will always remember the little shop in Manchester's Chinatown that sold the Jackie Chan books, direct from Kung Fu Supplies in Hong Kong. I wish I still had them. I had a glossy poster of Jackie in a gung fu pose on my bedroom wardrobe door from the same shop. Years later, the

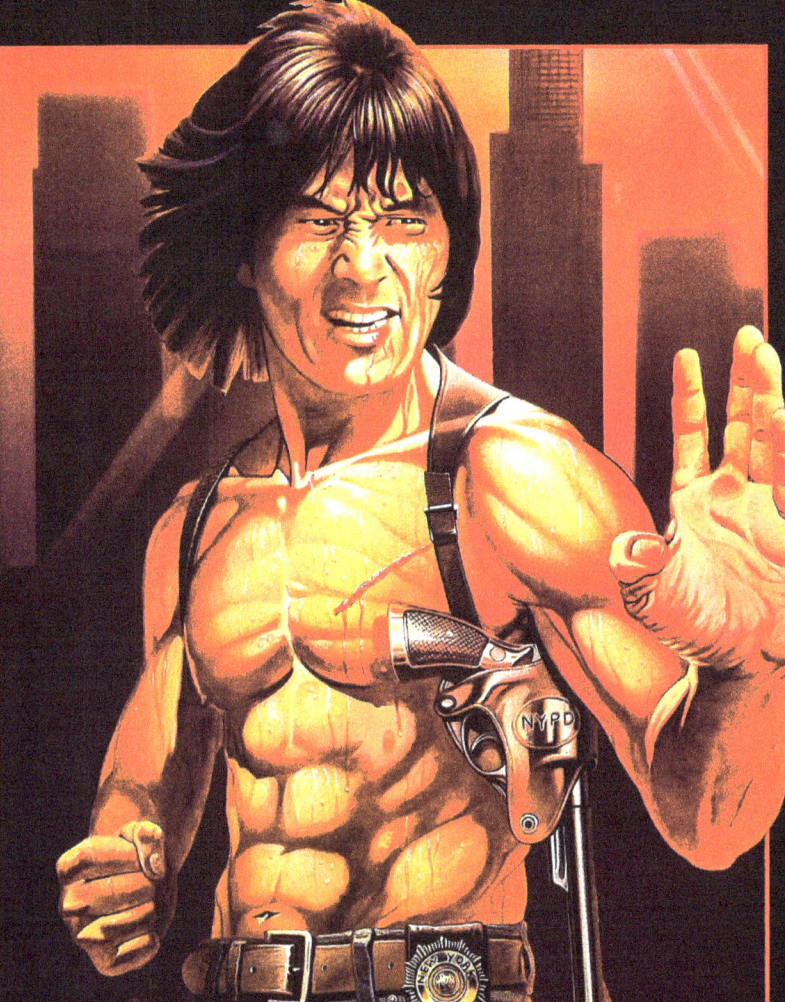

Blu-tack would ruin it, but I would always imitate the image of Jackie in his pose.

How good was "Project A"? Incredible, In fact, I might watch it again later! "Project A" hosted a plethora of Hong Kong stars, most notably of course was Jackie, Yuen Biao, and dai gor dai himself, Samo Hung. My rewind and fast forward buttons went into overdrive every time I watched this one. And I rented this favourite out repeatedly as it just had to be done. The superb bicycle chase scene is unforgettable, and of course, Jackie's homage to Harold Lloyd in the clock tower scene. Jackie worked incredibly hard to bring his own product to the audience. Gone were the tense, serious gung fu films for a more light-hearted approach to the genre. And the stunts...!! Oh my word. The essence of the clock tower stunt was seen and magnified in "Police Story." Not for the faint-hearted, I will never forget the outtakes as Jackie's character Kevin let out a shout like a Kiai before jumping onto the pole and descending down the lights, I can hear the crackling sounds now in my head. To my mind, there was no wire-fu in this movie. It has to be said, though, "Police Story" was definitely not like "The Protector," although I will watch both with slightly different hats on, to be fair. Again, my rewind and fast forward buttons were kept busy, more on "Police Story," less so on "The Protector." I just don't think you can beat the shopping mall fight scene in "Police Story" with the wall spring jump kick in the Gentlemen's club fight scene! That just pales in comparison with the excellent mall fight in "Police Story," I can watch that over and over as I am sure all fans can. I love the way Jackie does that scissor kick from the floor to make his opponent spin in the air! Everything in that crazy fight scene was pure perfection. If I had to introduce anyone to a Jackie Chan film, "Police Story" would be my go-to movie for sure. Never had I ever seen someone ride a motorbike into a glass display with a bad guy on the front wheel! Speaking of motorbikes, okay, let's be fair, the motorbike scene in Hong Kong harbour in "The Protector" wasn't bad at all.

JAMIE M. MACDONALD

Growing up with Jackie

Jackie Chan is adored by millions of fans worldwide, for me my love for Jackie started with two films: Snake in the Eagle`s Shadow and Drunken Master. Two action Kung Fu Comedies that still standout today, who would've thought that these two classics from 1978 would have the longevity that they have had, they really have stood the test of time., Yes I have countless versions from our shall we say recorded Rank VHS rental copies, to Made In Hong Kong sell through VHS, Hong Kong Legends DVDs, to the more recent Twilight Blu Ray release of both in the states, to Eureka Entertainment s release of Drunken Master in the UK, also 88films blu ray release of Snake in the Eagle`s Shadow. I adore both these films, but I have always favoured Snake in the Eagle`s Shadow. This film means so much to me, as a kid I would laugh, cry and watch in amazement at the physicality of Jackie. The physical comedy and slap stick humour is Universal and it clicked with young me so much. Comedy transcends cultural barriers and for me this is why these two films are still loved all over the world today!

Jackie turned seventy on the 7th of April this year just a week before my forty eight birthday; it amazes me to think that I have now being watching his films for forty plus years. From the early days of VHS in the late seventies to now, you could say that I grew up with him through his films. I love them all, really, like so many other fans I feel his seventies, eighties and early nineties films that are his best. I said above of my love for Snake in the Eagle`s Shadow, as a kid I watched daily, also some days more than once. I remember my cousin John and I watching these films, and making up our

own style; we called it the JJ Style. Looking back this still brings a smile to my face; we practised this every opportunity that we had. All learned from Chein Fu – Jackie`s character in the film. As he was learning so did John and I, it was great fun.

I was a very shy nervous kid whenever I was spoken to I would go bright red, also I had a stammer, I was nicknamed stutter rap. Kids can be very cruel, school at that time wasn`t a great place for me. I think the lessons taught to Jackie in the film through Martial Arts helped me overcome all these things, and that bullying time. Snake in Eagles Shadow showed me you can overcome things if you put your mind to it, you have to do for yourself, but Jackie Chan and Snake in the Eagle`s Shadow truly inspired me. I would like to say that I became a great Martial Artist, this was not my path. Instead I studied film editing which lead to me becoming a projectionist, which I still am today. Also, I review films and am hoping to become a writer for magazines,

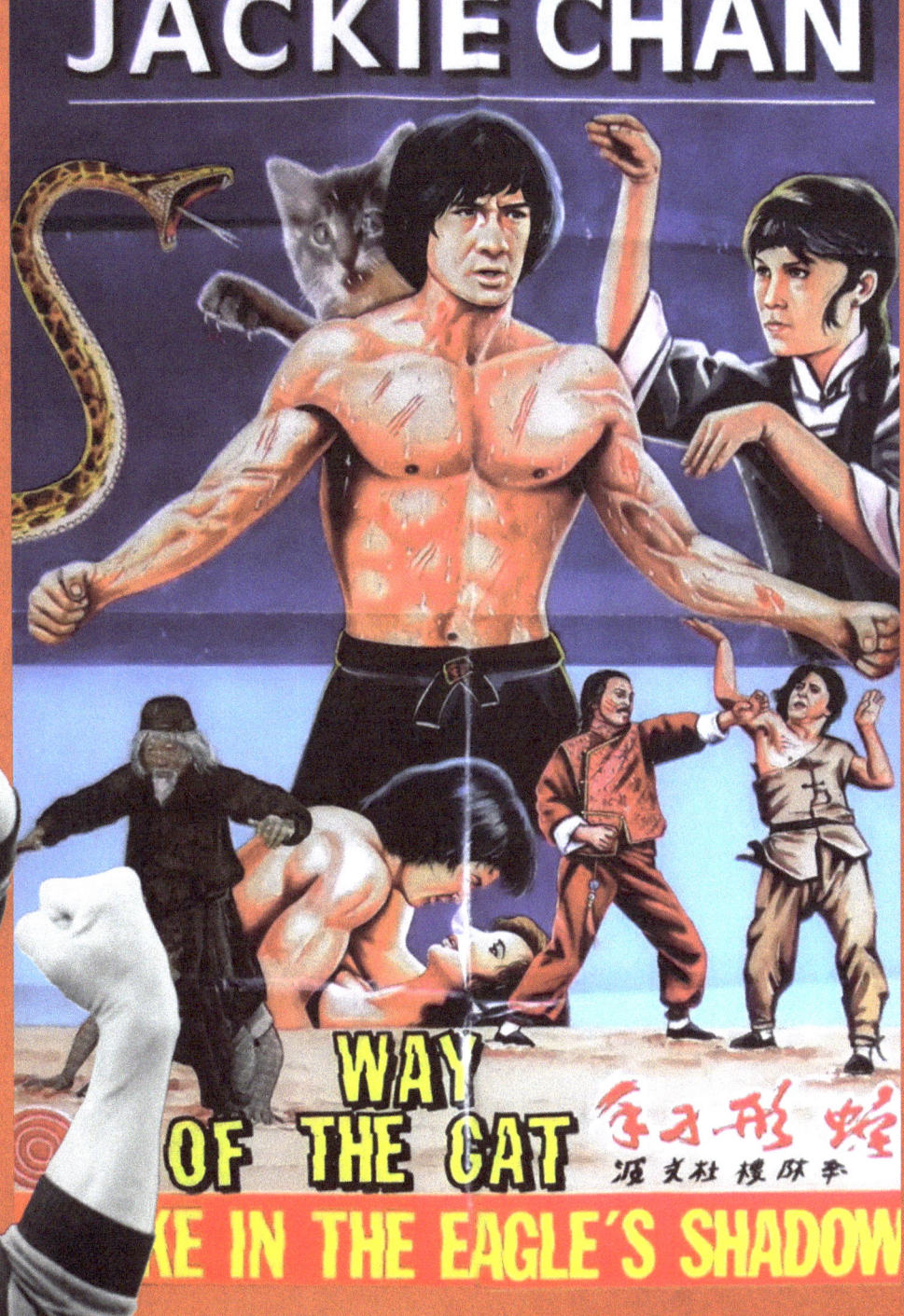

doing little pieces on the cinema, on the Martial Artists that I love. Why is Snake and Eagle`s Shadow still popular today, because like Buster Keaton and Harold Lloyd Jackie is timeless his comedies appeal to both the young and old. I honestly can`t wait to show my sons Snake in the Eagle`s Shadow and all the films I love of Jackie`s. I hope both Jackie himself and his films inspire them. One more thing, I would love to meet Jackie, which would be dream come true. My friend Phil did meet Jackie ten years ago, man that must`ve been awesome to meet your hero in person…

PHIL GILLION

We met Jackie Chan!

This was supposed to be called 'I met Jackie Chan' but something changed when I arrived in
China for Jackie Chan's 60th Birthday party for the " International Fan Club - Love, Peace and Friendship Tour 2014" something that amazed me, instead of it being about me, it became something bigger, something better, it became about us, the fans, the people that were there celebrating with me. I remember it well Monday 24th February 2014 that was the day I was sitting in my office and an email arrived, its header said 'Notice of Jackie Chan's 'International Fan Club - Love, Peace and Friendship Tour 2014' Now at the time I didn't really acknowledge it being more than some kind of communication so I opened it and was greeted by a message that said.

Dearest Jackie Chan Fan,

Congratulations!

We are very pleased to announce that you have been drawn as one of the lucky winners to participate Jackie Chan's "International Fan Club - Love, Peace and Friendship Tour 2014". This event will take place in Beijing and Shanghai between April 6 – April 10, 2014.

It was at that moment I screamed; no, I did, the actual realization that I had won a competition to meet Jackie Chan started to sink in, not only that but as part of his 60th Birthday celebrations. The shock came as it

was literally only two weeks earlier I had entered the competition to meet Jackie Chan it was straight forward send your name and address and My Story with Jackie Chan (write a story about you and Jackie Chan, or your aspirations for Jackie) so I wrote;

As a Jackie Chan fan since the age of 12, some 30 years ago I watched in awe at this man that changed my outlook on Chinese movies and have since followed Jackie through his career watching every film with avid fascination and I still get the same childish excitement today in watching Jackie Chan Movies.

The above still holds true today. So everything was paid for by Jackie we just needed flights, about 900 fans worldwide gathered and our first stop was Beijing and 17 coaches were put on with me being in coach Number 4 or 'lunchbox number 4' as we have called ourselves.

Things happened so quickly, we did go to a Jackie Chan Love, Peace and Friendship Concert in Beijing that I remember as being rather surreal as hundreds of fans were waiting for a sight of Jackie outside the venue and screaming and we were all ushered in as special guests. The amazing thing happened along the way to meet Jackie is that I was with likeminded people from across the globe that loved Jackie so it was like talking with friends we had some much in common because of our love for Jackie Chan and or his films that instant friendships were formed, in fact lifelong friendships were formed.

Then we went to the Jackie Chan Fans party where we met the man himself it was one of the most exciting and emotional experiences of my life after watching Jackie on film for 30 years to actually meet him was a dream come true. (and yes he loved my T-shirt)

Tiananmen Square and The Forbidden City

So many stories that so many people will tell for me, it was an experience of a lifetime for others too. On the train to Shanghai we joked about how we should write something profound about the whole experience and I didn't have a clue, that is until Jody gave me a sweet and inside the wrapper was this quote "*Satisfy your sense of surprise*" WOW Surprised, 100% satisfied thank you, more than that Thank you to each and everyone I met on the trip (Angie, Stephen, Glen, Ben, Sharaz, Jody, Alison, Ling, Karl william the list goes on) who made that experience more than just how I met Jackie Chan, but actually how………………… We met Jackie Chan. Find Phil at www.easternfilmfans.co.uk and on social media.

AN ODE TO 快餐車

WHEELS ON MEALS

By Chris Grant

'And now gentleman, all for one, one for all - that is our motto, is it not?'
-Alexandre Dumas, The Three Musketeers

I have regularly written about my love for Jackie Chan, his movies and all things Hong Kong Cinema. It was delightful when Eureka followed up the release of my masterpiece, Project A, with one of the greatest films ever made - *Wheels on Meals*.

Wheels on Meals is the second film showcasing The Three Dragons (made up of Hong Kong superstars Sammo Hung, Yuen Biao and Jackie Chan) and they are the perfect on screen trio. The film, set in Barcelona, follows brothers Thomas and David (played by Chan and Biao) successfully running a mobile eatery. Through a series of events they become embroiled with their old friend Moby, a failed private eye (played by Hung), and they team up to solve a suitably ridiculous case.

When The Three Dragons are together on screen the results are magical: on the one hand you have wondrous slap stick comedy, the quality of which is reserved for the likes of Laurel and Hardy and on the other hand you are treated to the kind of on screen physical prowess of Buster Keaton. The standard here is impeccable and the frenetic pace has the film moving from one astonishing set piece to the next creating a hugely enjoyable 95 minutes.

The final act of *Wheels on Meals* is one of the best in cinematic history. We see The Three Dragons infiltrating a castle to recuse the captives and are witness to one of the most thrilling action sequences ever filmed. This has affectionate nods to to the Ritz Brothers version of The Three Musketeers while combining the physical comedy of Harold Loyd's Safety Last. The results are thrilling: The real showpiece of the film is a one on one fight between Benny 'The Jet' Urquidez, a real life kick boxer with a towering record of 63 professional wins and no losses, and Jackie Chan.

I believe this is the greatest fight sequence ever filmed: starting slow and building into an absolute frenzy of skill. It is a masterclass in film making and performance. It has been referenced countless times and is an action sequence that has never been topped. It represents a style of film making that doesn't

exist anymore, particularly in the main stream, where the physical acts performed on screen are the special effect.

It is common place for actions films to be defined by their CGI spectacle. Go to your local multiplex and the latest CGI riddled super hero movie will be there to be 'enjoyed' likely stating it has more bang for buck than the last. These massive spectacles of robots smashing into each other, harshly edited with frenetic jump cuts and riddled with banging sounds and explosions are common place now. There is no integrity involved: these films are made for today and designed to be forgotten tomorrow. Wheels on Meals is a homage to the days of cinema when Gene Kelly would film a 30th take to ensure the dance sequence in Singing in the Rain was perfect, when Bela Tarr would wait by his camera all day to ensure he got the perfect opening shot for his masterpiece Damnation or when Stanley Kubrick shot 60 takes of Jack advancing towards his victim in The Shining ensuring he had the perfect shot; It is this dedication that creates perfection like *Wheels on Meals*, a film to be embraced, savoured and remembered.

FRANK DJENG
Talks Jackie Chan
Interview by Simon Pritchard

SP: Hi Frank and welcome. Thank you for choosing three of the films you have done commentary for us to discuss today.

TWIN DRAGONS

SP: So, the film was a fund-raising project?

FD: Yes, it was a fundraising film for the Hong Kong Film Directors Guild so that they can buy a new location so that they can build a building. *Twin Dragons*, or *Twin Warriors*, I hate the retitling, by the way! So, everybody who worked for Twin Dragon literally worked for free to keep the film's budget down. The budget was a little bit over $1,000,000 US. But the main thing was to keep the costs down and that's why you also have people like Ringo Lam and John Woo and Tsui Hark directing it.

SP: The film introduces the two different Jackies, what are your thoughts on them?

FD: The one is kind of like a little mini gangster or gangster wannabe, I sometimes think that Jackie sometimes uses these opportunities to showcase his real personality. You know, like when I look at the gangster role, I always thought that there's a little Jackie in there. Similarly, like in *Dragons Forever*; Jackie is also kind of a womaniser. Sometimes I look at it like, wow, maybe he is like a womaniser in real life because obviously we all heard rumours about having girlfriends like Maggie Cheung, you know. Sometimes I would feel that you know some of his films have got to have reflected a part of his real personality. I think that having him playing this gangster in *Twin Dragons* kind of gives him an opportunity to just be who he really is sometimes, you know, a little bit goofy, a little bit playful, a little bit womanising, that sort of thing. But the jealous guy is more like a regular Jackie.

SP: The gangster Jackie teams up with Teddy Robins. For the people who don't know of Teddy, who is he please?

FD: Teddy is great. Teddy is really a legend in the Hong Kong film industry. He's also a Twin Dragon executive producer and one of the story contributors. Teddy started in the 1960s and he was in a rock band in Hong Kong. He formed a band with his friends called Teddy Robin and the Playboys. He

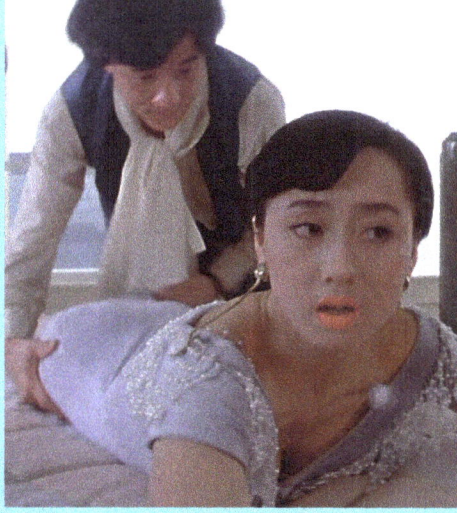

was the vocalist and guitarist, and his band was really the first Chinese band in Hong Kong that played English rock. They were popular until the 1970s.

Teddy switched careers to movie producing. He joined Cinema City and starred in and produced all those fantastic comedies directed by John Woo and Tsui Hark and starred with George Lam in films like *All the Wrong Clues* and *Banana Cops*, but he continued to release music. He was also one of the few Hong Kong artists to have done a concept album, similar to a Pink Floyd album. He did an album called '*Man from Outer Space*', which is a concept album and it's great! Is it just a continuous, almost like 40 minutes of non-stop music with songs and just music so you know that's unheard of for Hong Kong at that time. But then of course, most people know him as an actor, comedian, he is rather distinguished, he always dubs his own voice because once again people know his voice so well from his singing. So, it's almost like he hasn't got a choice which he always does, which is great. I was so pleased that I got to meet him in Hong Kong a few years ago at a film premiere. I was beyond myself because he's one of my idols. He's still working. He's still doing films and stuff, so he is really a pretty critical figure in the Hong Kong entertainment industry for about 60 years now.

SP: The female roles played by Maggie Cheung and Nina Li. What are your thoughts on their roles and the interaction with the two Jackies?

FD: Maggie is more cultured and she's more civilised. She's the classic female love interest, whereas Nina Li is more of a goofball. Nina Li, I think gave her best performance in her career in this film. She's obviously a throwback to these actresses from Hollywood in the 1930s, like the kind

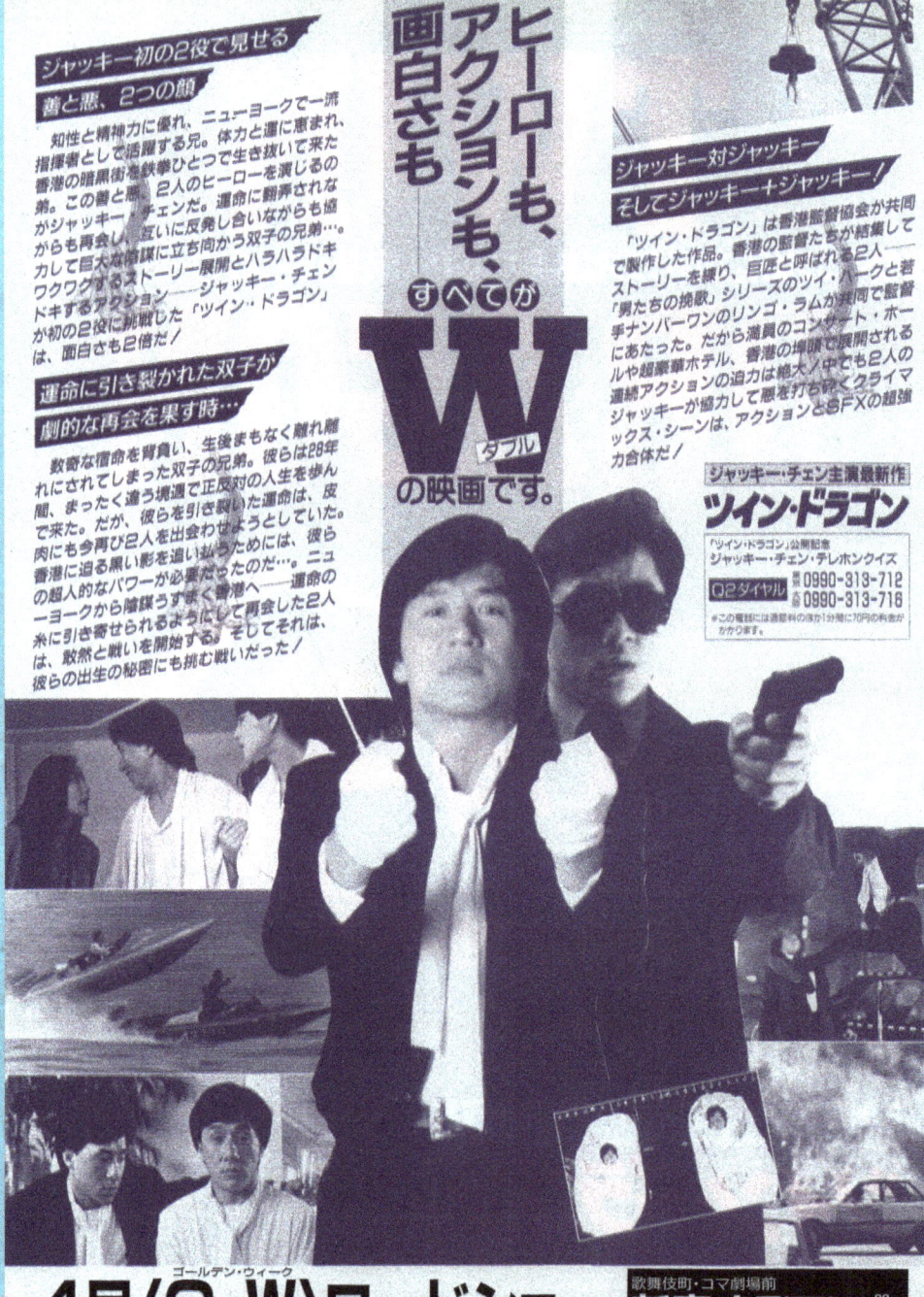

you see in Bob Hope Films, The Marx Brothers, that sort of thing. I love that, but she's obviously there to contrast with Maggie, just like the brothers in Jackie. You have these contrasts with the two ladies. One more playful and goofier and the other, more earthbound. It's also continuing the screwball comedy theme where you have multiple relationships going on, and of course you have two Jackie's. Obviously, you can't just have one actress and that increased the comedic impact of the film to have somebody like Nina, who's willing to kind of go all out and do all this.

SP: The speedboat scene existed and there was a lot going on..

FD: So, there's one thing we missed discussing in the commentary, because I didn't find that out until afterwards, the speedboat chase was actually shot by John Woo. John Woo was using this boat scene as a rehearsal for the boat chase that he would eventually shoot in 'Face Off'. He already knew that he was going to do another Hollywood film as this was made when he had finished 'Hard Target'. He was about to do 'Face Off' and of course this film being a fundraiser, he used it to try out his idea and rehearse. When you watch 'Face Off' you can see the similarities in the way that the whole thing was edited together with the high-speed rhythm.

SP: One of the best scenes, especially for the time, was the hot tub scene. It was filmed brilliantly, the speed at which the different Jackie's switch between each other, and it builds up and becomes more frantic. I noticed the lack of technology at the time only really when Jackie pushed 'his' nose

and the other time when he pushed 'his' chest; the rest was good, the criticism seems a little harsh. What do you think?

FD: Oh, I love it. It's a great homage, not just the screwball comedy, but also the French farce, you know. Jackie always has French farce elements in his films, *Project A* or even *Armour of God*. I mean it takes a lot of takes to make these scenes work flawlessly. It's a perfect example of his homage to those genres. Of course, some of the visual effects are a little bit rough, but you know it's the idea that matters. I mean, as a viewer, you know that it's impossible to have two Jackie Chans in real life, so it must be done by optics. It doesn't matter if the optics aren't perfect. Now you have the beauty of blu-ray, if you look at that scene a little more carefully, you notice some of the shots involving the two Jackies, one of the Jackie was actually doubled by Mars. That's how creative they were, and they're using every trick of the trade to make that scene work. It is also an obvious way to save money, they can't have optics throughout the entire scene, right? Like hey, whatever works. And that scene worked.

SP: It was nice to see Teddy again at the end hanging from the crane, was that him?

FD: I mean who else could double Teddy!? Look at his dedication to his work. Like I mentioned, you have one of the most important figures in the Hong Kong music and film industry hanging from a crane.

SP: I'd like to think the Jackies ended up with their opposites at the wedding, you?

FD: Yeah, I think it would have been a great idea to have the opposite Jackie getting the girl like you said, Nina getting the nice Jackie and not realising it, and then Maggie getting the gangster. To pull that off, I think they would have had to come up with a way to let the audiences know that they've switched, but that the two ladies don't know, I mean to make that work right? But I think that would have been a great idea to have them switched. Maybe have the gangster Jackie turn to the camera, break the fourth wall, and wink at the audience as he walks away with Maggie.

ARMOUR OF GOD

SP: There is a great Indiana Jones and the Temple of Doom theme initially in this film.

FD: Yeah, I think the idea was to have the entire film inspired by Indiana Jones but because of his injuries, they had to change. They could not have Jackie doing a lot of these adventurous stunts anymore because they worried that he would become ill, and he would get injured again. I mean, with that opening scene, it's obvious that they were doing the Indiana Jones rip off and then also going on that adventure to find an artifact, all that stuff. But then once Jackie hurt himself and he recovers, they said "you know what? We can't do that anymore, you must change the storyline a little bit." That's why I mention in my commentary that halfway through the film, it became a James Bond film. He became to act like a

spy, instead of being on an archaeologist type adventure. He became kind of like a spy agent in finding out what's going on, but I think it was a necessity for them to change direction. So that's why whenever I watch *Armour of God* now, I have a feeling like the first half is *Indiana Jones*, the second half is James Bond where he goes to the enemy's den and stuff.

SP: The enemy's den at the end and the monks and their occult, reminds me of the Hammer Horror films like 'T*o the Devil a Daughter*' and '*Devil Rides Out*'. What are your thoughts?

FD: I have to be honest with you. I'm not really a horror fan. I mean, I like sci-fi horror. I'm a big fan of the Alien and Predator series or horror films with comedy, like Mr. Vampire. To me the finale is more like James Bond, and the cave is more like Sean Connery going to the volcano in "You Only Live Twice", that sort of thing.

SP: For the benefit of those that do not know, how did Jackie suffer the potentially life-threatening injury during the filming of *Armour of God*?

FD: He thought that a tree can support his weight and fell I think maybe between 10 to 20 feet at the most, landing and piercing his skull on a rock. So, Jackie did the stunt twice before he said "OK, let's do it a third one". He wasn't satisfied with the first couple of takes because that scene was about the tribes that were supposedly chasing him, and he just felt that they were not chasing him hard enough. Jackie wanted it to be more convincing. And of course, the problem was while you were doing all those practice takes, the tree got weakened by him grabbing and swinging it. And so, by the time he did the third and last take, the branch broke and that's how he fell.

SP: The film then goes to H.K. and introduces a band called "The Losers" that are a parody of a successful band called the "The Winners".

FD: Yes, that was Alan Tam's actual band, "*The Winners*" that is and because of this, Eric Tsang wanted to kind of make fun of

him. So that's why they call the band "The Losers". That was just a little quick little in-joke/parody thing.

SP: The film is aimed at both Jackie Chan and Alan Tam fans, and we're billed equally. Can you please explain who Alan Tam is and the popularity of him at the time?

FD: Alan was as big as Michael Jackson. Alan is Hong Kong's version of Michael Jackson. For those of you who grew up in the 1980's, you know how big Michael Jackson was. Alan achieved that by doing hundreds of concerts in Hong Kong. He was doing nonstop solo concerts for a month at the Hong Kong Coliseum because tickets were just kept selling. There's just such a high demand for tickets. Alan was also in the "The Winners" and then he went solo. He and the other lead singer in "*The Winners*", Kenny Bee both went solo, but Alan's success was much bigger.

Alan started releasing albums in the late 1970's, but it was in the early 1980's when he did three back-to-back albums in 1984 alone. And all three albums were huge hits. That led to this superstardom of Alan. He was big throughout the 1980's and winning awards after awards until the late 1980's. And that's when he said, "you know what, I'm not going to accept any more awards". Alan kept winning all these awards, Best Singer, Best Song and all that stuff to the point where no one else was winning them. This is not healthy for the industry because there was no competition. So, around 1988 or 1989, he stopped accepting awards. By the early 1990's, the fans had grown up. I mean the craze was pretty huge. That's why maybe Western audiences wouldn't understand how come you have a double billing with Alan as Jackie's equal. But once you know, for those of us who grew up at that time, and remembering how Big Alan Tam was, we understand that it has to be that way. It has to be double billing. Also, the fact that the film's Chinese title is called "Dragon and Tiger Brothers". So right away with that title, you know you have to have them as equals.

SP: I must mention the car chase scene. Who created it?

FD: Rémy Julienne. He was Hollywood's go-to vehicle stunt coordinator. He did the Italian Job and several James Bond films. That's what I mean by the James Bond references again. Like, if you look at the car chase, it's straight out of "For Your Eyes Only" and so they went all out to have this international calibre of cars, stuntman, action directors, to go in and do these chases so that the film looks more like an international production than Hong Kong production.

SP: You say that Cynthia Rothrock was lined up to the main fight at the end of this film. How come that never came to fruition?

FD: Well, yes, the end was supposedly a fight between Jackie and Cynthia Rothrock. Jackie was going to fight the leader of the cult and Cynthia was going to be the leader, the ultimate villain, but because of his injury, the film was postponed for close to a year, so Cynthia then couldn't do it due to her contract with the studio and filming commitments, so they ended up having the Amazon women fighting Jackie, with some of the Amazon women actually played by male stuntmen. If you watch closely, you can tell some of them were guys from Jackie's stunt team in wigs.

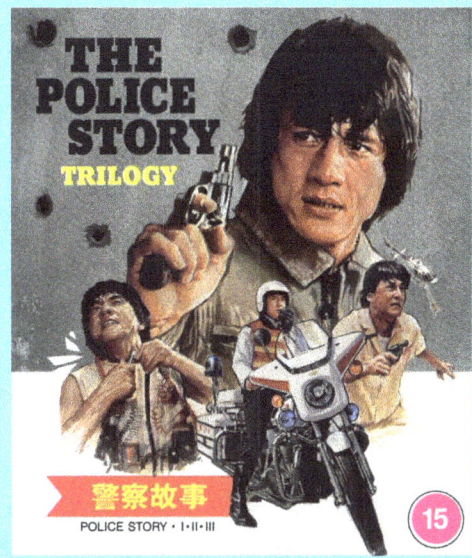

POLICE STORY

SP: After "*Battle Creek Brawl*", "*Project A*", "*Cannonball Ball Run*" and "*The Protector*", Jackie goes all out to break the USA. With hindsight, how influential do you think this film has been in the West?

FD: It was influential in Hong Kong mainly for incorporating action in the modern setting because prior to "*Police Story*" the majority of Jackie's action films were set in ancient China or early 20th century China, like "*Dragon Lord*" and "*Young Master*". Due to his involvement with "The Lucky Stars" series, he realised he can do the same thing but set in modern time, and that's how we got the "*Police Story*" films. "*Police Story*" came about because he was so dissatisfied with his experience working on "*The Protector*". Jackie felt his hands were tied; his suggestions and opinions weren't appreciated. He didn't like how it came out. He thought 'you know what, I'll do one better, I'll do "Police Story" to show you how it should really have been done'. "*Police Story*" was concocted at a time when he failed to put a dent in Hollywood after making "*Cannonball Run*", "*The Protector*" and "*Battle Creek Brawl*" and all three films didn't do that. I mean, *Cannonball Run* did well in the US. but it's not because of Jackie and it didn't even help him break out to the market. I mean people remember him, but he's in a small role. "*Battle Creek Brawl*" was specifically made to get him into the American market. It didn't work for the reasons that I talked about in the commentary. "*The Protector*" was just like any other goofy cop drama that people saw in the US back then, so it's kind of ironic that it takes Jackie's own Hong Kong film to break him into the West later. Especially with "*Rumble in the Bronx*", which is, in terms of film, not as good as "*Project A*" and "*Police Story*", but it was really Rumble that kind of brought Jackie back into Hollywood. So, to me, from the Western perspective, *Rumble in the Bronx* was more influential for Jackie Chan's breakout in Hollywood than "*Police Story*".

SP: You talk about how this film was used at the time for H.K. police department for recruitment and propaganda, they even use one of Jackie's speeches. Can you please tell us about this?

FD: The Royal Hong Kong police at that time decided to use his image from "Police Story" as their marketing material. Obviously, they had to get Jackie to agree to it and I think Jackie was fine with it. You have to remember this was a time when Hong Kong police was still well regarded by the general Hong Kong public. This sort of changed after the 2019 demonstrations, which will take us days to talk about, but back then Hong Kong police had been positively received by the Hong Kong public for a long time; especially during the 1980's and 1990's because of all the portrayal of cops in the TV series. It was only natural to have the Hong Kong police use Jackie as a role model to promote recruitment.

SP: The film has a strong start; the destruction of the Shanty town was on an epic scale and what makes it look even better now is, none of it is CGI. How did they do this?

FD: "*Police Story*" was filmed in 1985 and that was the time when there were quite a lot of these, not illegal, but really not safe establishments dating back to after World War 2, where houses were built on metal plates or wood panels. These can easily cause fire because of how hot Hong Kong is and because of people's carelessness in starting fires, like maybe when they're cooking and stuff. The Government decided to get rid of these houses. The Government was trying to replace them with high-rise residential buildings and so these little places were being demolished one by one.

When Jackie found out that the Government is about to demolish this shanty town area, this squatter's area, Jackie asked "well, can you let us destroy it?", the Government said "Sure, do with it what you want".

That's why they set that scene in that area and Jackie was able to kind of go all out with these cars running down the hill. It was not a set; it was an actual town where people used to live there for decades.

SP: We have to mention the bus scene. One thing about this I loved about this scene was the stunt crew and Jackie swinging in and out of the bus windows fighting whilst it was moving. If you'v ever put your hand out the window of a moving vehicle, that wind pressure is strong, the element ofdanger in this stunt is amazing. The umbrella part is iconic.

FD: They had to use steel or metal for the umbrella and the handle, you know, so that it wouldn't break. I mean if you just use a regular umbrella, it would have had to stand Jackie's weight and the pressure. You can tell that's just him holding on to it. There're no wires. How can you put wires on a moving bus? You can't right? I think in the outtake there was one shot where he almost fell out of the bus. Jackie obviously had his stuntman inside the bus to watch him and make sure that if he falls, they can get to him right away. But no, there're no wires. It's just that umbrella made of metal.

SP: At the end of the scene one of the stuntmen that comes through the top of the bus window breaks their neck, what happened?

FD: I think he might have been paralysed. They missed their queue and the bus stopped short as they were supposed to land on the top of the car, but they just fell to the cement. The bus driver panicked and braked prematurely.

SP: The film has so many cameos from film stars to H.K. T.V. stars. The amount you can name is incredible. At one point you mention the T.V. show appears on and that it is an actual H.K. T.V. show, so the attention to detail is crazy. Who is your favourite cameo in this film?

FD: Oh boy, I think Michael Lai (Music composer) was my favourite cameo. Also, people like Sandy Lam and a couple people like that were in this film. It is fun to spot the cameos. Jackie loved to have these little cameos and so for local people who know these celebrities, it's nice to spot them.

SP: The end Mall scene is one of the most famous Jackie scenes. In your commentary, not only do you talk about Jackie's caution in jumping, but the voltage going through those light bulbs. What was that about please?

FD: He was…well, he was scared. He was more nervous about jumping. He didn't even think about the fact that he could have been electrocuted, you know, cause of course, Hong Kong being Hong Kong the voltage is 220. The UK is 230v isn't it? but yes, the USA is only 120v. So right away the voltage was already high, but also the fact that he was sliding down a metallic rod surrounded by these electric light bulbs. Oh yeah, he could easily be electrocuted, but he didn't even think about that. They were just worried about Jackie injuring himself from that slide because you have to remember he is not just sliding down; he also must hit that little canopy thing and have to break through it. The concern was that he would get physically injured, but not by electrocution. Jackie hesitated in jumping until near 3:00 AM. I think everyone was like waiting for him to jump. They had to give the shopping mall back to the operators soon, because the shopping mall had to open in the morning. They were shooting that throughout the night because that's when the shopping malls are closed and by the time they got to the part where he has to jump, you know they were telling him "Look, Jackie, you know we got to do this because it's almost dawn". They also needed time to clean up the place so that they could get the mall back to the operators. I think it was around 3:00 AM whenhe finally decided, "I'm going to do it" and that's why in the scene you saw him yelling, he screamed first before he jumped. That was his way to give himself the courage to jump.

SP: Which ending of this film do you prefer, Hong Kong or Japanese?

FD: Japanese. The Hong Kong ending stopped on the freeze-frame of him beating up Chor Yuen, but in the Japanese ending, we saw them outside the mall afterwards. You see him getting led away by his boss and then he turned around and saw Maggie. Maggie turned around. And then Bridget was there and all that stuff. So that's in the Japanese ending. I felt he probably wouldn't get arrested because of him being a cop, but he was in kind of trouble because of the damage he's done to the whole mall, so they had to take him away or something. The Japanese ending was better in my opinion, it felt more complete. Again, it's Jackie being Jackie, showing that both girls fall for him, I mean it implies that Bridget also may have some feelings for him, and Maggie obviously does, being his girlfriend. It's a typical cop movie ending where you know, I mean the good guy and the good cop was led away, that sort of thing. I think this was the better ending, so I do prefer the Japanese ending. It gives it a nice little conclusion to the plot. I always like to see plot lines in the film getting resolved at the end.

SP: Thank you for taking time to speak with me again. What have you come up with next?

FD: FJ and I just finished recording commentary for PROJECT A Parts 1 and 2, both coming out on 88 Films. Those are coming in the summer at the earliest, I think. The boxset for both films has been delayed because they were finding more new stuff to put in it. So that's why it's been delayed. I also finished doing commentaries for Eureka's THE VALIANT ONES for 4K UHD, and THE MIRACLE FIGHTERS Blu-Ray, and 88 Films' FIST OF LEGEND and BODYGUARD FROM BEIJING 4K UHDs. I'm still doing a whole bunch of commentaries for other labels like Vinegar Syndrome, Shout Factory and Arrow and I'm about to start doing commentaries for Arrow's Shawscope Volume three box. Our Bruceploitation documentary ENTER THE CLONES OF BUCE will be released on Blu-ray in the UK on 27th May 2024. Further releases are coming, and we have not one, but TWO huge Bruceploitation boxsets coming soon, so we're proud of that. Thanks, Simon, it was a pleasure talking to you.

FANATICAL DRAGON PRESENTS
5 FINGERS OF DISCS

Written by Johnny Burnett aka *The Fanatical Dragon*

It's been quite some time since I had a chance to dive into the latest Jackie Chan Bluray releases here at Eastern Heroes, so somewhat fittingly for this 70th Anniversary special issue, we have a healthy stack of pretty special JC physical media releases to take a look at, including a few that may well be of much interest to our American based friends (and to those outside the USA with a multi region player!)Let's begin with the highest profile label release of the recent crop…

Jackie Chan : Emergence of a Superstar
Criterion Collection
Region A Bluray
USA ONLY
OUT NOW

Criterion finally turn their attention to incorporating more of Jackie's back catalogue into their collection and what a random mix of titles they have picked to do so with! This 4 disc boxset pulls together several Lo Wei era titles : *Spiritual Kung Fu*, *The Fearless Hyena* and it's rather questionable sequel *Fearless Hyena 2* and *Half a Loaf of Kung Fu* then adds in *My Lucky Stars* and the *Young Master* to round out the set. For those of us in the UK, we have had excellent versions of almost all of these thanks to 88 Films and Eureka, but for the US market, this is a pretty great release of some 'maybe not as great as others' Jackie movies. But the extras Criterion have put together for the set do somewhat make up for the titles they've selected for the release… We get 2K digital restorations of *Spiritual Kung Fu*, *The Fearless Hyena*, *Fearless Hyena II*, *The Young Master*, and *My Lucky Stars* and a high-definition digital restoration of *Half a Loaf of Kung Fu* all with uncompressed monaural soundtracks as well as Alternate stereo and 5.1 surround Cantonese soundtracks. They've been able to also include the Classic English-dubbed tracks for *Half a Loaf of Kung Fu*, *Spiritual Kung Fu*, *The Fearless Hyena*, and *Fearless Hyena II*, plus an English-dubbed alternate track for *Fearless Hyena II* as well as Contemporary English-dubbed tracks for *The Young Master* and *My Lucky Stars*.

We get brand new audio commentaries for *The Fearless Hyena* and *The Young Master* from Frank Djeng aka the Master of Remaster aka The Commentary Beast.

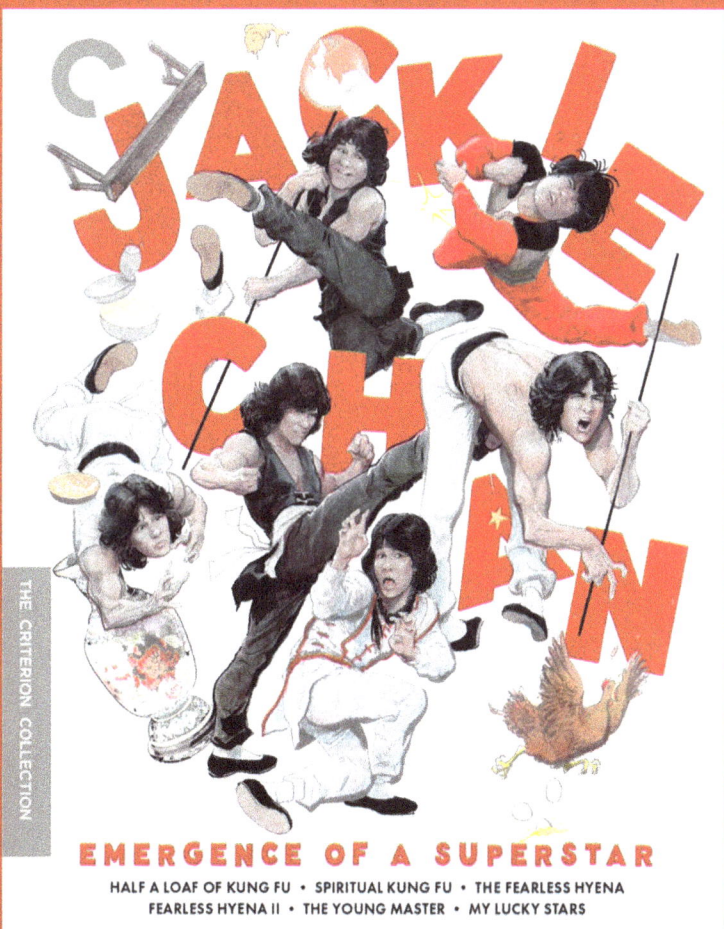

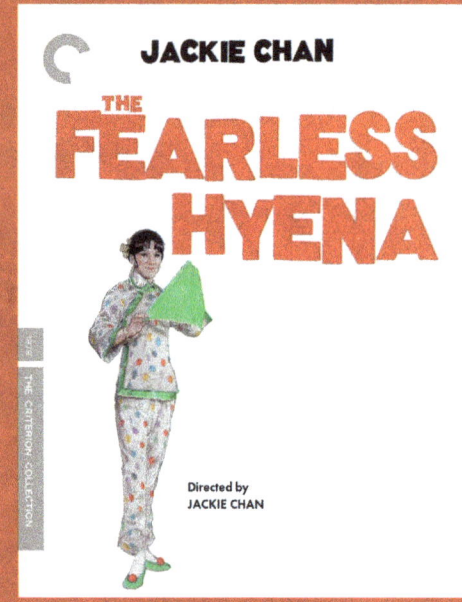

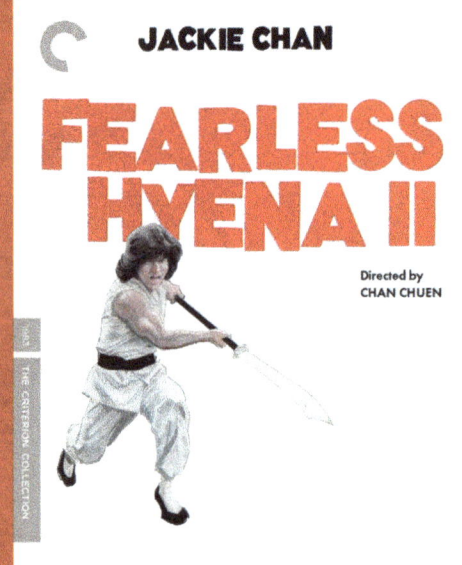
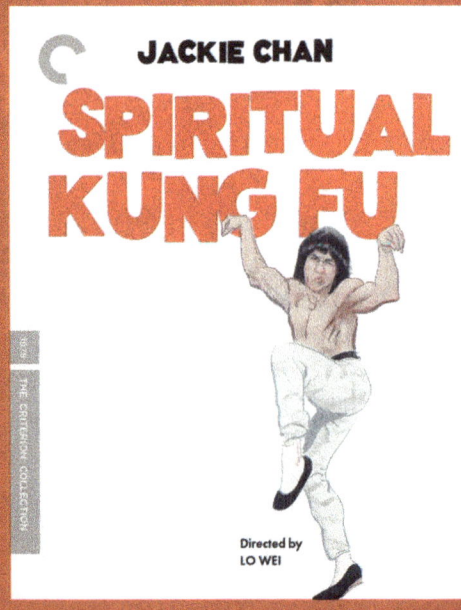
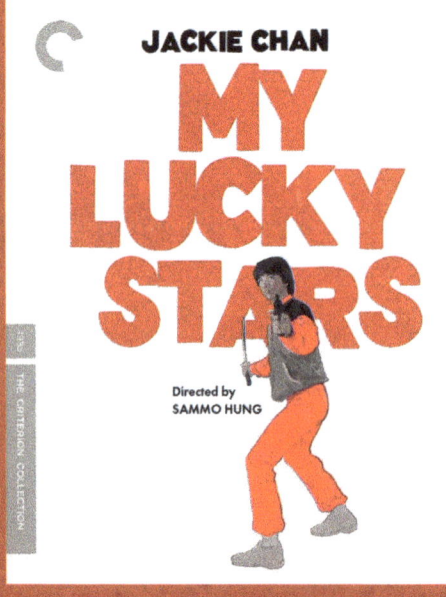

A new Interview with author Grady Hendrix (These Fists Break Bricks) about actor-director Jackie Chan. Archival interviews with Chan, actor-director Sammo Hung, actors Michiko Nishiwaki and Hwang In-shik, The Young Master promo reel from the 1980 Cannes Film Festival and deleted scenes from the film. A archive Interview from 2005 with Hong Kong cinema critic Paul Fonoroff about producer-director Lo Wei, NG shots from The Young Master and *My Lucky Stars*, Trailers as well as newly updated English subtitle translations (courtesy of Frank Djeng) and an essay by Alex Pappademas. The cover art for the set is by Kyle Baker Whilst I would have much preferred Criterion to pick other titles than the ones they've opted to go with here, it's great that the USA is getting another solid Jackie Boxset, though when held up against the two Shout Factory sets we'll look at later in the article, this one maybe isn't quite the success it could have been..

Fearless Hyena 2
88 Films
Region B Bluray
MAY 2024

For those of us in the UK lamenting the lack of *Fearless Hyena Part 2* release here, 88 Films are set to bring out the film here in Late May. Always a title that receives much debate from Jackie fans as ti it's relative merits or sins, give it's troubled production and Jackie leaving midway through filming to defect to Golden Harvest forcing Lo Wei to finish the movie with recycled footage and stand ins. It's a curious oddity amongst Jackie's filmography, one i'm not much of a fan of but many, many fans are. 88 are giving it the special edition treatment and also bringing back fan favourite cover artist Kung

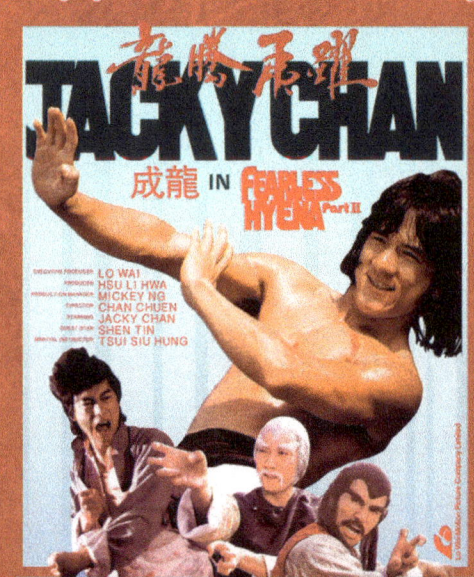

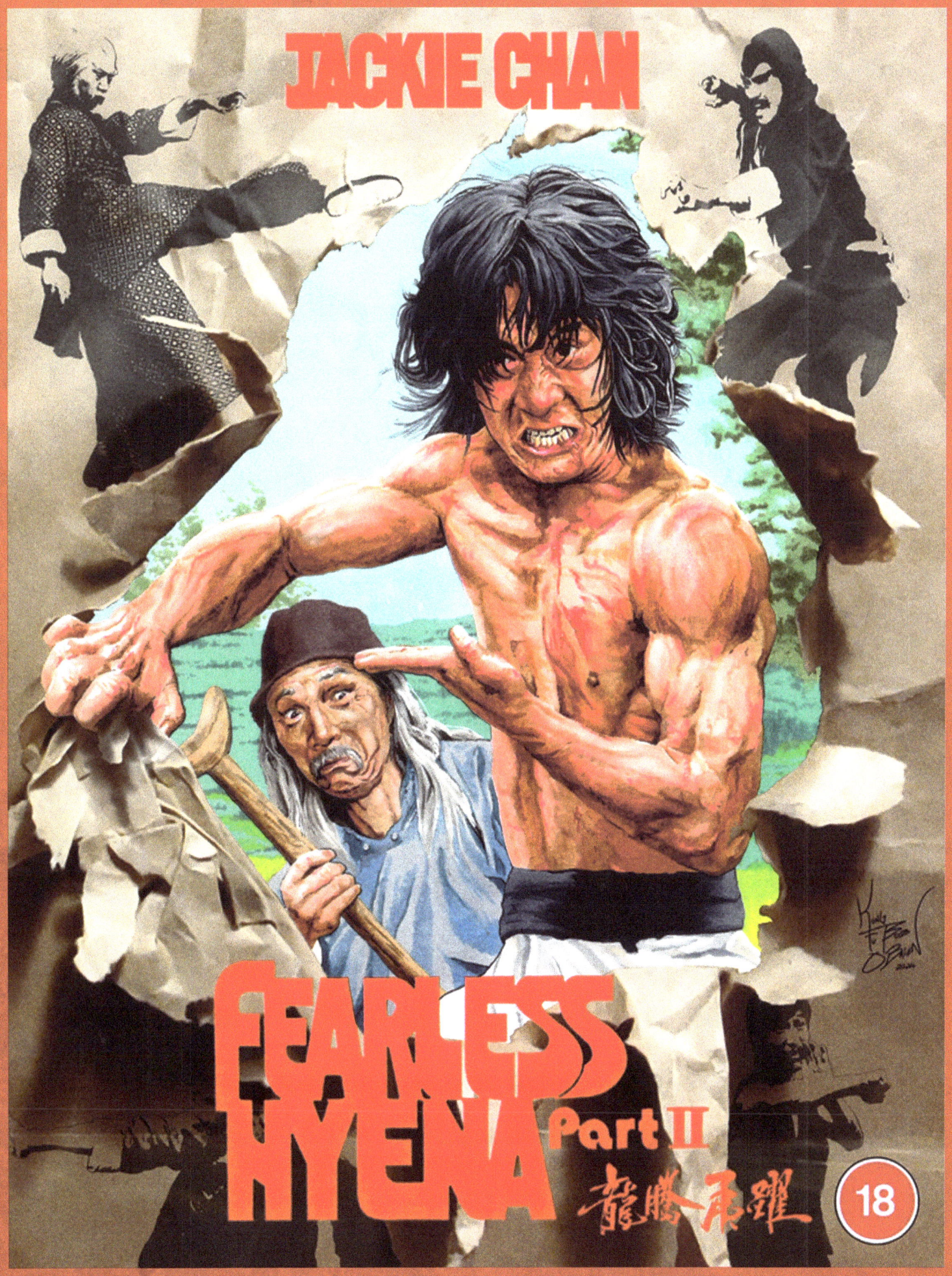

Fu Bob O'Brien to make an excellent piece of art for the from of the box and slipcover. Frank Djeng has recorded a (different to his Criterion track) audio commentary for the release and 88 films have sourced the original Cantonese audio and two English dubs for the film.

Battle Creek Brawl Collectors Edition
88 Films
Region B Bluray
OUT NOW

Sticking with 88 Films, I haven't had a chance to feature their recent re-release of Battlecreek Brawl, Jackie's first real attempt to crack the US market. Pairing him up with enter The Dragon director Robert Clouse. 88 released this years and years ago now, but it's been given the limited edition treatment with an all new (much, much better) 2K remaster from the original negatives. We get an 80 page booklet, poster and six reproduction lobby cards, two audio commentaries - one from Frank Djeng joined by FJ Desanto and a second track from film critic Kim Newman and Barry Forshaw. Archive interviews with Jackie and Golden Harvest head honcho Raymond Chow as well as featurettes from David West and a short titled *Rumble in the USA* - Jackie takes on America with our very own Ricky Baker. Kung Fu Bob once again steps up for cover art, poster and sketch duties, and does a pretty amazing job, it's a glorious piece of cover art, which makes the included poster all the sweeter.

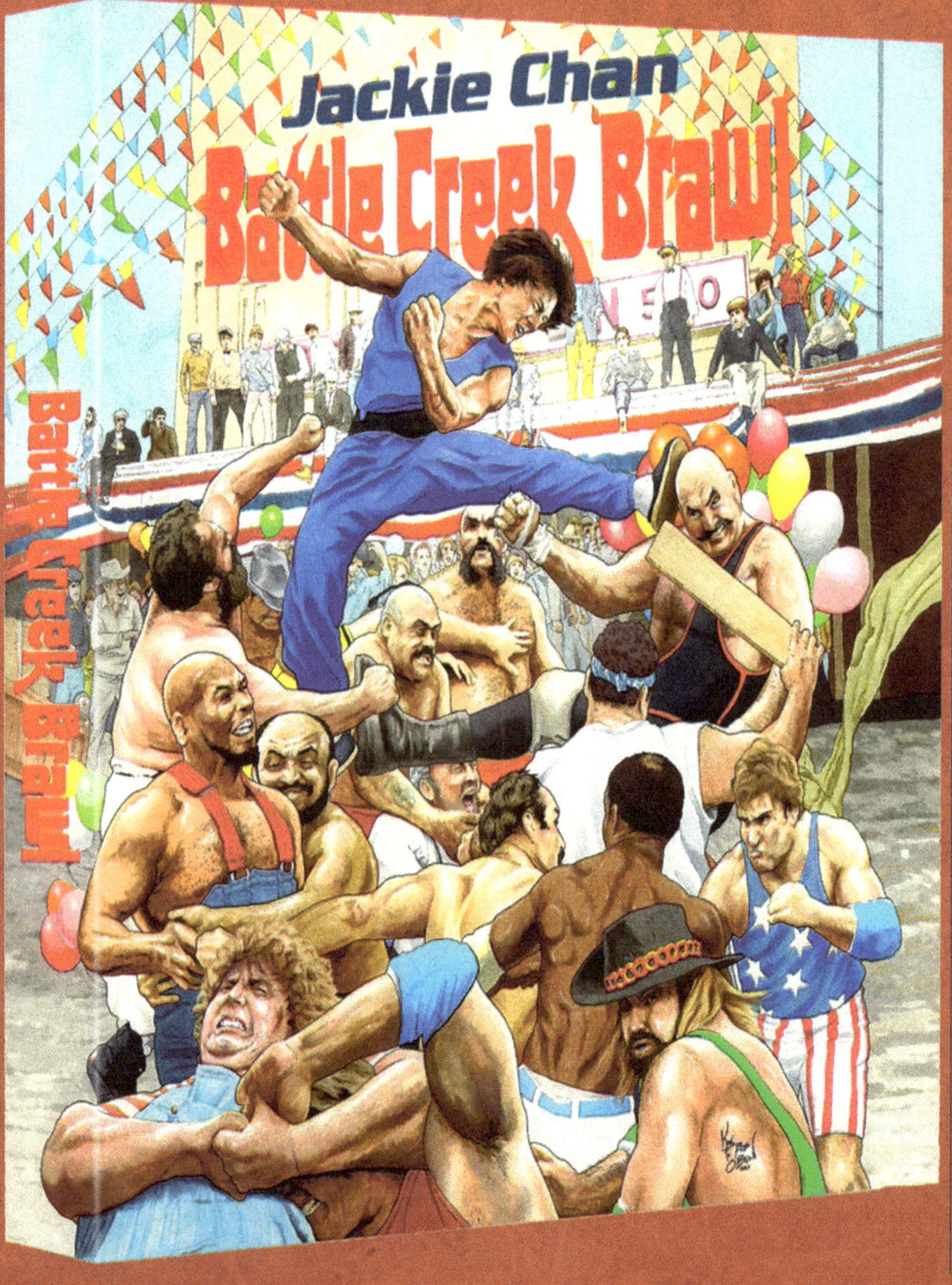

Ride On
CIneAsia
Region B Bluray
OUT NOW

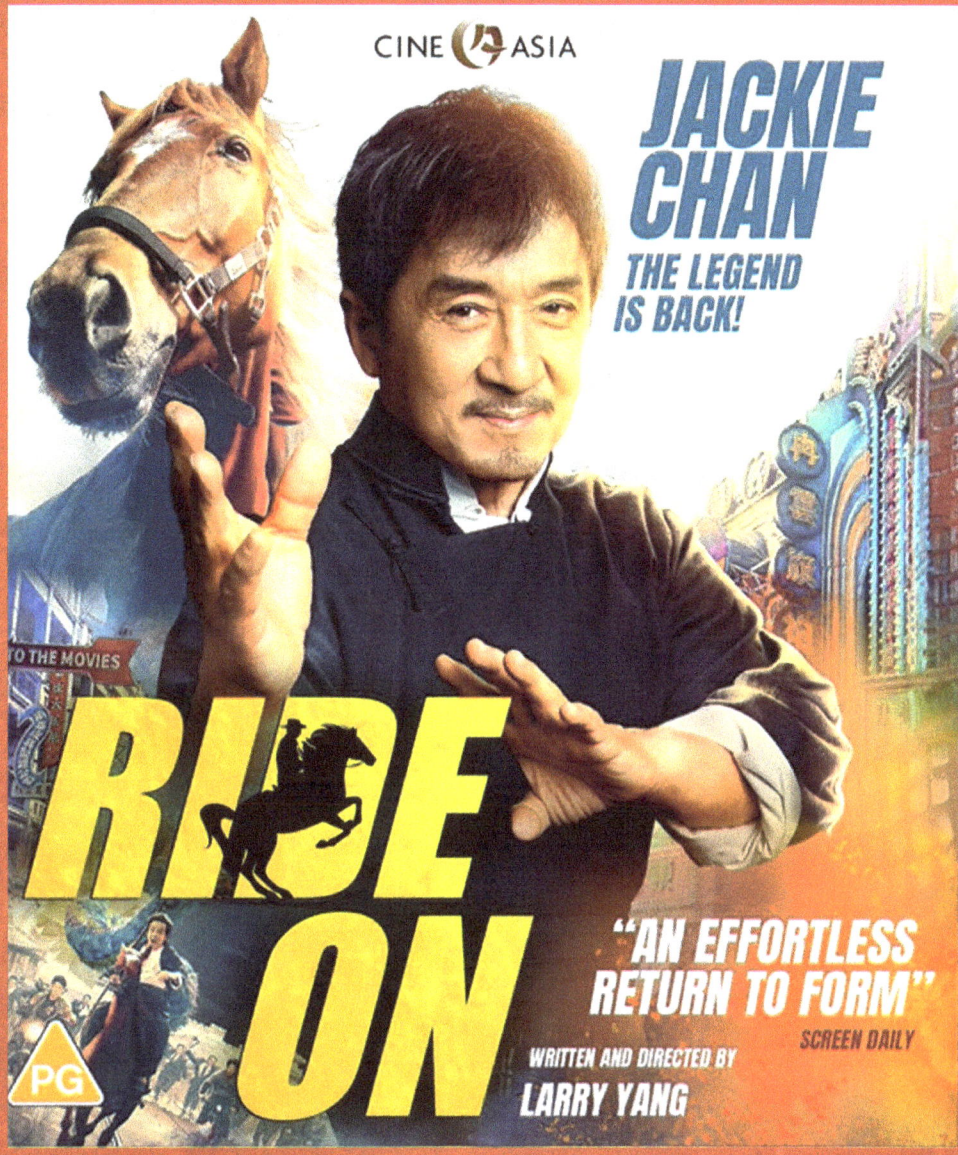

Cine Asia also fairly recently released to Bluray (and DVD) Jackie's most recent cinematic outing (here in the UK at least) Ride On. The disc is pretty much bare bones but the film was a great return to form of sorts for Chan. being received more favourably than *Vanguard* or *CZ12* were by his fanbase. The synopsis provided by Cine Asia reminds us that: Chan plays Luo, a washed-up stuntman whose glory days are far behind him. When his trusty stunt horse, Red Hare, becomes the target of debt collectors, the pair fight off the attackers, with their impressive display caught on camera and the video going viral. Meanwhile, Luo works to reconnect with his estranged daughter and her boyfriend, who both take an interest in the legal case against Luo. But when his renewed fame scores him a once-in-a lifetime opportunity, will he finally put his family first?

Whilst it would have been nice to have a more features loaded disc, we should be grateful that Cine Asia are working hard to bring us NEW Chinese and HK movie titles. The Boutique labels all tend to focus on movies made a long, long time ago, and whilst this is great, there is also a space that desperately needs to be filled for new releases, if we don't keep supporting current Chinese and HK movies, they'll stop making them available to us outside of China!

Project A & Project A Pt2
88 Films
4K/Bluray combo and Region A Bluray Only Editions.
USA ONLY
OUT NOW

Saving the best 88 Films related news for last (last from 88 films for now anyway)

The UK based Label have secured the rights to bring out a 4K UHD release in the USA of Jackie's classic *Project A* and *Project A Pt2*. This will be an American only release (Eureka Entertainment still hold the rights to the UK market for the two films) But from all the releases covered here in this issue, this is THE one well worth importing to the UK (most 4K discs are region free, for the Bluray set, you will need a multi region player)

As with Battle Creek Brawl, This will come as a limited edition boxset, likely loaded with extras. Kung Fu Bob once again has delivered a slice of solid gold for the cover of the set. Extras are still being worked on at the time we were going to print, but already confirmed are a brand new 2024 interview with Mars (who famously did that clock tower high fall ahead of Jackie doing it) A bound book (expect 80 pages or more) Six repro Lobby Cards and a poster. We also get what looks like all the old Hong Kong Legends archival extras, and given that they were HUGE DVD releases for HKL back in the day, the extras produced for the two Project A movies back then were substantial, it's great to see them being ported over. I would be astounded if we didn't get at least one Frank Djeng and FJ Desanto

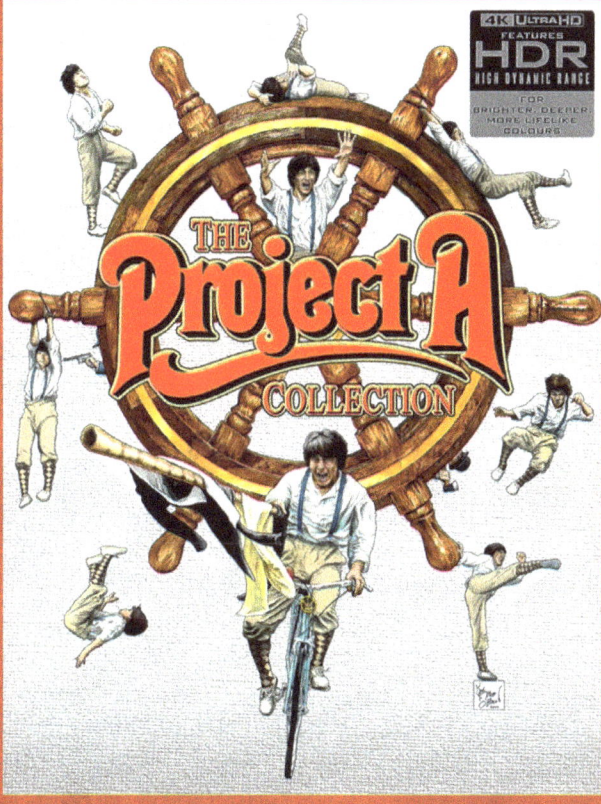

audio commentary for each movie and presumably much, much more. It's expected to drop sometime in July.

For any not familiar with the movies (if that's possible!) Here are the two synopsis for the movies…

PROJECT A
Dragon Ma (Jackie Chan, Rush Hour) is a lieutenant in the 19th-century Hong Kong marines. Pirates have been terrorizing local waters, with assistance from the corrupt authorities. Dragon Ma hopes to defeat the evil pirate clan led by Sanpao (Dick Wei), but his plan is short-circuited. Ma then teams with a navy admiral (Hak Suen Lau), a police captain Tzu (Biao Yuen) and a crafty thief (Sammo Hung) in a new round of high-seas battles with Sanpao and his pirates.

PROJECT A: PART II
Corrupt police inspector Chun (David Lam) has made himself the most powerful law enforcement officer in Hong Kong by staging high-profile arrests of the criminals and mobsters with whom he's in cahoots. The British authorities know Chun is a dirty cop but have not been able to infiltrate his inner circle. Enter fearless and incorruptible military policeman "Dragon Ma" Yun (Jackie Chan), who comes back to his hometown to pose as Chun's new right-hand man and take down both cops and criminals. 88 Films did an absolutely incredible job with their previous 4K releases of Police Story 3 and Dragon's Forever, i don't doubt they'll absolutely smash it out the park for Project A!

The Jackie Chan Collection, Vol. 1 (1976 - 1982)
Shout Factory
Region A Bluray
OUT NOW

Probably the biggest two releases Stateside for Jackie Chan films in the past two years have come from Shout Factory, jumping firmly on the HK Physical media Bandwagon with impressive gusto, we've looked at several of their Shaw Brothers boxsets in other issues. They've released Donnie Yen's *Tiger Cage* series and across Two sets have pulled together a pretty sizeable bunch of titles previously only available outside of the States from 88 Films and

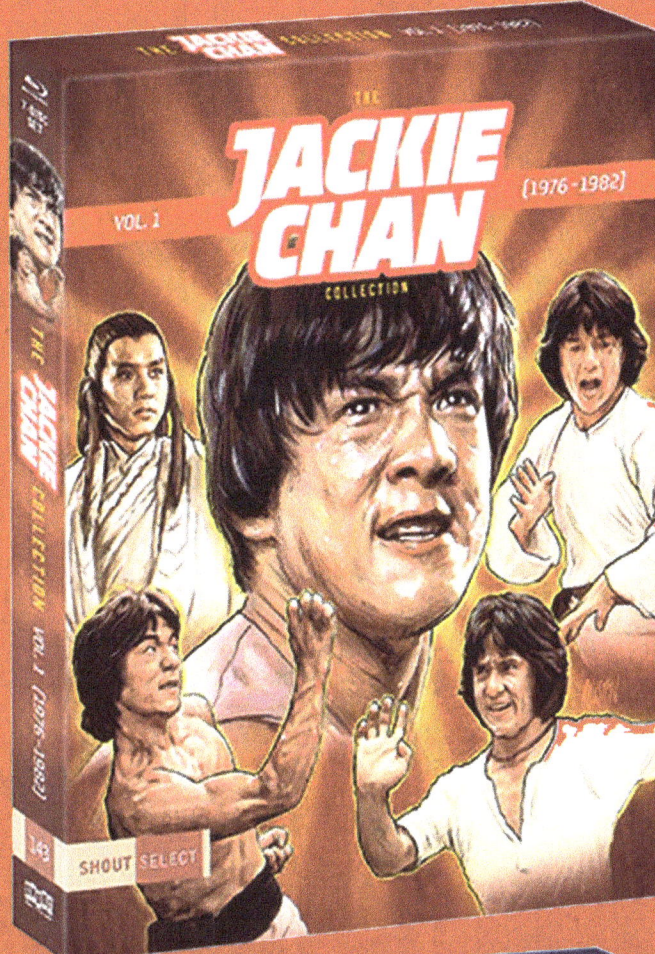

Eureka here in the UK and from a few European labels. Volume 1 covers the period between 1976 and 1982 and pulls together 7 movies. *The Killer Meteors* (one of Jackie's rare turns as a villain, squaring off against Jimmy Wang Yu), *Shaolin Wooden Men*, arguably the best of Jackie's Lo Wei era movies, *To Kill With Intrigue*, *Snake and Crane Arts of Shaolin*, *Dragon Fist*, *Battle Creek Brawl* and *Dragon Lord*. Shout have put together a pretty exceptional package of extras for the boxset, including a host of film specific interwith our own glorious leader Ricky Baker, Ricky's interviews cover *Shaolin Wooden Men*, *To Kill With Intrigue*, *Snake And Crane Arts of Shaolin* and *Battle Creek Brawl*.

There are also Audio commentaries for each film, some by David West and some from James Mudge a variety of TV spots including a wealth of Japanese TV trailers and spots across all seven movies.

The Jackie Chan Collection, Vol. 2
(1983 - 1993)
Shout Factory
Region A Bluray
OUT NOW

Volume Two brings us firmly into Golden Harvest territory and gives us 8 movies in total. *Winners & Sinners*, *Wheels on Meals*, *The Protector*, *Twinkle Twinkle Lucky Stars*, *Armour of God* and it's sequel *Operation Condor*, *Crime Story* and *City Hunter*.

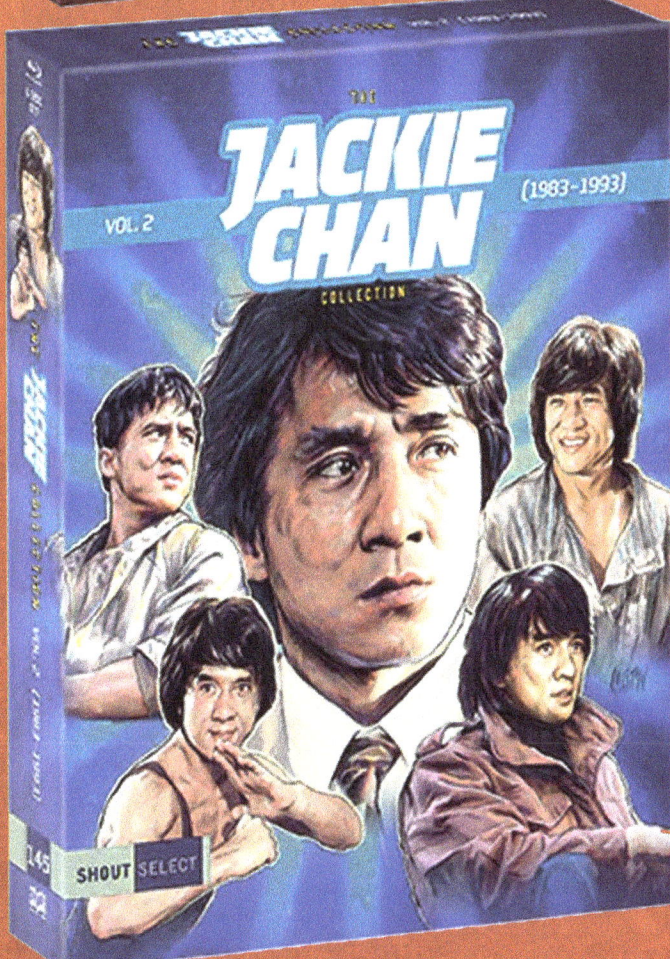

Again we get all new commentaries for all eight films, with David West and James Mudge sharing the duties (individually) across the movies. a stack of archival interviews with various cast and crew and most intriguingly for Volume 2, An extra titled, Break-Neck Brilliance: A New Era Of Jackie Chan And Skeleton-Shattering Stunts – An 88-Minute Feature Length Documentary On How Chan Broke The Mold (And His Bones) With His Daring Choreography And Set Pieces Upon His Return To Hong Kong In The 1980s, Featuring Interviews With Wang Yao, One Of The Original Members Of The Jackie Chan Stunt Team, Emma Lee, Former Manager Of Talent For Golden Harvest, Chi-Hwa Chen, Executive Director Of Police Story, Vincent Lyn, Actor In Operation Condor, Academic Dr Lin Feng, Frank Djeng Of The NY Asian Film Festival, And More…

It's great to see the USA getting their own releases of the early era JC movies and even more so, the classic Golden Harvest era epics, but for me the biggest reason to be cheerful amongst these is Project A making it's way onto 4K!

You can be sure we'll be covering that release in depth right here in Eastern Heroes when the time comes in a future issue but for now, please find me over on Youtube for loads more Physical Media, news, film reviews, unboxings and more!

www.youtube.com/thefanaticaldragon

JACKIE CHAN
THE STUNTMAN WHO BECAME A LEGEND
By Rick Baker

Jackie Chan, the name synonymous with action-packed entertainment, has captivated audiences worldwide with his unparalleled blend of martial arts prowess, comedic timing, and death-defying stunts. But behind the glitz and glamour of his blockbuster hits lies a story of resilience, determination, and sheer grit—a journey that began long before he rose to prominence as a leading actor.

Born Chan Kong-sang on April 7, 1954, in Hong Kong, Jackie Chan's early life was marked by hardship and struggle. His parents, Charles, and Lee-Lee Chan, worked gruelling jobs, to make ends meet, leaving young Chan to fend for himself much of the time. At just seven years old, he was enrolled in the China Drama Academy, a rigorous institution where he would spend the next decade honing his skills in martial arts, acrobatics, and traditional Chinese opera.

It was during his time at the China Drama Academy that Chan's talent for performing and his fearless demeanour caught the eye of the legendary filmmaker and martial artist, Bruce Lee. Chan was cast as a stuntman in Lee's 1972 film, "Fist of Fury," marking the beginning of his illustrious career in the world of cinema. Despite his brief appearance in the film, Chan's natural agility and fearlessness left a lasting impression on Lee, who encouraged him to pursue a career in the film industry.

Following his stint with Bruce Lee, Chan began working as a stuntman and bit player in a series of Hong Kong martial arts films. His early roles were often unaccredited, and he frequently found himself risking life and limb performing dangerous stunts for little pay and recognition. But Chan's relentless work ethic and unwavering commitment to his craft soon caught the attention of filmmakers, and he began to receive more substantial roles in a variety of action films.

It wasn't until the mid-1970s that Chan's career began to gain traction, thanks in part to his collaboration with director Lo Wei. Under Wei's guidance, Chan starred in a string of successful films, including "New Fist of Fury" (1976) "snake & crane Arts of Shaolin" (1978), which showcased his unique blend of martial arts prowess and comedic flair. However, it was his partnership with director Yuen Woo-ping that would ultimately catapult Chan to international fame.

In 1978, Chan teamed up with Yuen Woo-ping for the classic martial

arts comedy "Drunken Master." The film was a commercial and critical success, earning Chan widespread acclaim for his innovative fight choreography and comedic timing. It also marked the beginning of a fruitful collaboration between Chan and Yuen, who would go on to work together on several more films, including "Snake in the Eagle's Shadow" and "Drunken Master II."

Despite his growing popularity in Hong Kong cinema, Chan's breakthrough into the international market came with his role in the 1978 film "The Big Brawl." Although the film received mixed reviews, it helped to raise Chan's profile outside of Asia and laid the groundwork for his eventual success in Hollywood.

Throughout the 1980s, Chan continued to build his reputation as one of the most bankable action stars in the world, starring in a string of box office hits such as "Police Story" (1985) and "Armour of God" (1986). But it was his role in the 1995 film "Rumble in the Bronx" that solidified his status as a global superstar. The film, which was Chan's first major American production, showcased his trademark blend of jaw-dropping stunts and comedic timing and became a surprise hit at the box office, grossing over $32 million in the United States alone.

Since then, Chan has continued to thrill audiences with his high-octane action sequences and infectious charm, starring in a diverse range of films spanning multiple genres. From the heart-pounding thrills of the "Rush Hour" series to the heart-warming drama of "The Karate Kid" (2010), Chan has proven time and again that he is more than just a martial arts icon—he is a versatile actor capable of captivating audiences of all ages and backgrounds.

Today, Jackie Chan's influence extends far beyond the realm of cinema. He is not only

an accomplished actor and filmmaker but also a philanthropist, UNICEF Goodwill Ambassador, and cultural ambassador for his native Hong Kong. His tireless dedication to his craft, and his unwavering commitment to giving back to his community have cemented his status as a true legend of the silver screen.

In conclusion, Jackie Chan's journey from humble beginnings to international superstardom is a testament to the power of perseverance, hard work, and self-belief. Through sheer determination and an unyielding passion for his craft, Chan has defied the odds to become one of the most beloved and enduring figures in the history of cinema. And although his early years as a stuntman may have been fraught with danger and uncertainty, they ultimately laid the foundation for a career that would inspire generations of moviegoers around the world.

THE DYNAMIC DUO

By Rick Baker

In the realm of buddy cop comedies, there's one duo that stands out among the rest: Jackie Chan and Chris Tucker in the iconic "Rush Hour" series. Directed by Brett Ratner, this action-packed franchise not only catapulted Jackie Chan to global superstardom but also redefined the buddy cop genre with its winning combination of martial arts action and laugh-out-loud humour.

The inception of "Rush Hour" can be traced back to the late 1990s when director Brett Ratner was looking to create a fresh take on the buddy cop formula. Inspired by the success of films like "Lethal Weapon" and "48 Hrs.," Ratner envisioned a high-energy action-comedy that would appeal to audiences of all ages. Enter Jackie Chan, the martial arts maestro whose charisma and stunt expertise were already legendary in the world of cinema.

Chan's involvement in "Rush Hour" marked a significant milestone in his career. While he had achieved considerable success in Hong Kong and had made a splash in Hollywood with films like "Rumble in the Bronx," "Rush Hour" propelled him to a whole new level of international fame. His chemistry with co-star Chris Tucker, who played the fast-talking Detective James Carter, was electric, and their on-screen banter became the heart and soul of the franchise.

The first instalment of "Rush Hour" hit theatres in 1998 and was an instant hit with audiences and critics alike. The film followed the unlikely partnership between Detective Inspector Lee (Chan) from Hong Kong and Detective Carter (Tucker) from Los Angeles as they joined forces to rescue the kidnapped daughter of a Chinese diplomat. Packed with adrenaline-pumping action sequences and side-splitting comedy, "Rush Hour" struck a chord with viewers around the world, grossing over $244 million worldwide.

One of the most remarkable aspects of "Rush Hour" was its seamless integration of Jackie Chan's trademark martial arts prowess with Brett Ratner's slick direction and Chris Tucker's comedic timing. Ratner's dynamic approach to filmmaking, coupled with Chan's unparalleled stunt work and Tucker's larger-than-life personality, created a winning formula that resonated with audiences of all backgrounds.

The success of "Rush Hour" paved the way for two equally entertaining sequels: "Rush Hour 2" (2001) and "Rush Hour 3" (2007). In "Rush Hour 2," Lee and Carter find themselves in Hong Kong investigating a counterfeit money scam, while "Rush Hour 3" sees them teaming up once again to thwart a global crime syndicate. Both films delivered the same winning combination of action and humour that made the original a smash hit, further solidifying the franchise's place in cinematic history.

Behind the scenes, Jackie Chan's dedication to his craft and his commitment to performing his own stunts added an extra layer of authenticity to the "Rush Hour" films. Despite the risks involved, Chan insisted on doing many of his own stunts, including the jaw-dropping fight sequences and death-defying leaps that have become his trademark. His fearless approach to filmmaking not only raised the bar for action cinema but also endeared him to fans around the world.

In addition to its entertainment value, the "Rush Hour" franchise also broke new ground in terms of representation and diversity in Hollywood. By featuring a Chinese protagonist in a leading role and showcasing the vibrant cultures of both Hong Kong and Los Angeles, the films helped to broaden the scope of mainstream cinema and pave the way for greater inclusivity in the industry.

As we look back on the legacy of "Rush Hour," it's clear that the collaboration between Jackie Chan, Brett Ratner, and Chris Tucker has left an indelible mark on the world of cinema. From its pulse-pounding action sequences to its laugh-out-loud comedy, the franchise continues to entertain audiences of all ages and backgrounds, proving that when it comes to buddy cop comedies, there's no duo quite like Lee and Carter.

MEMORABILIA

A TANGIBLE CONNECTION TO THE WORLD OF JACKIE CHAN
BY EMILIO ALPANSEQUE, CALIFORNIA, USA

In the early 80s, a homemade VHS tape of Snake in the Eagle's Shadow, obtained from a local Chinese restaurant, sparked my interest in this film and in everything related to it. It led me to follow Jackie Chan's career, practice martial arts extensively through all my life, love martial arts cinema and Chinese culture, become a writer and staff reporter for a few martial arts magazines worldwide, and eventually meet Jackie in person, interview him multiple times, and more. Of course, collecting all sorts of Jackie Chan memorabilia became a cherished hobby of mine ever since.

Over the years, without being extremely organized nor overly obsessed, I have managed to accumulate a large collection of Jackie Chan-related items, including (but not limited to) the following:

JACKIE CHAN
RUMBLE IN THE BRONX
JC Interviews 3
JACKIE CHAN
BEST FIGHTS AND GREATEST STUNTS
成龍
MOUTAI
CHENGLONGJIU
FITNESS
KUNG FU YOGA
MAGNIFICENT BODYGUARDS
PROJECT A
RUSH HOUR

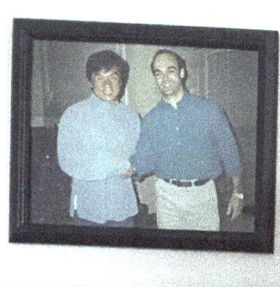

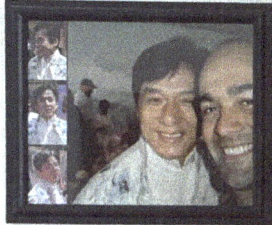

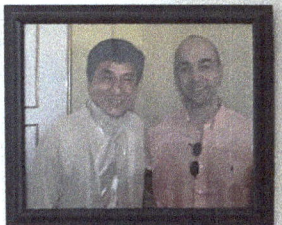

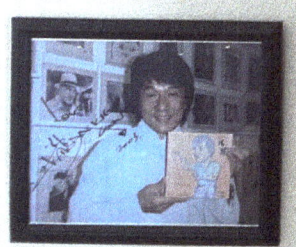

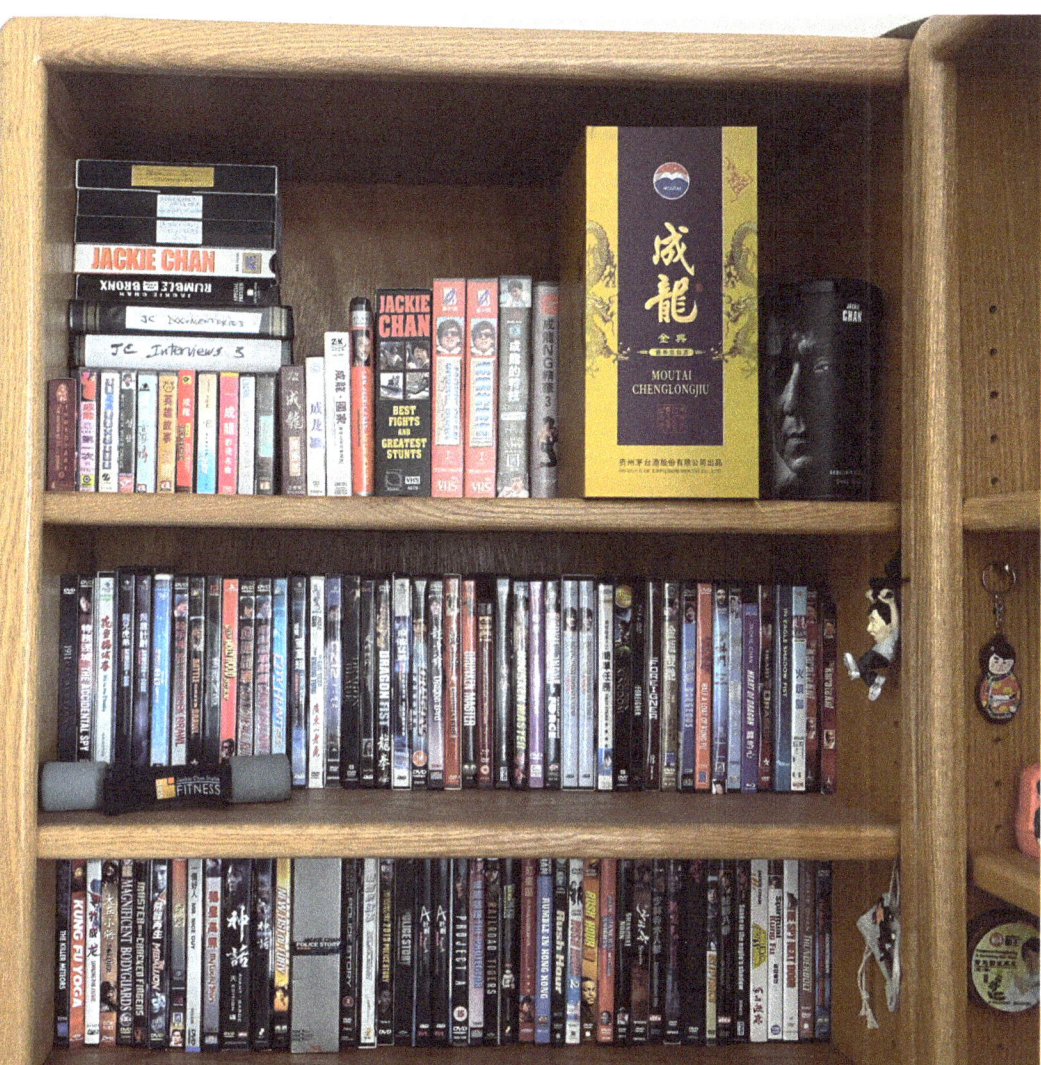

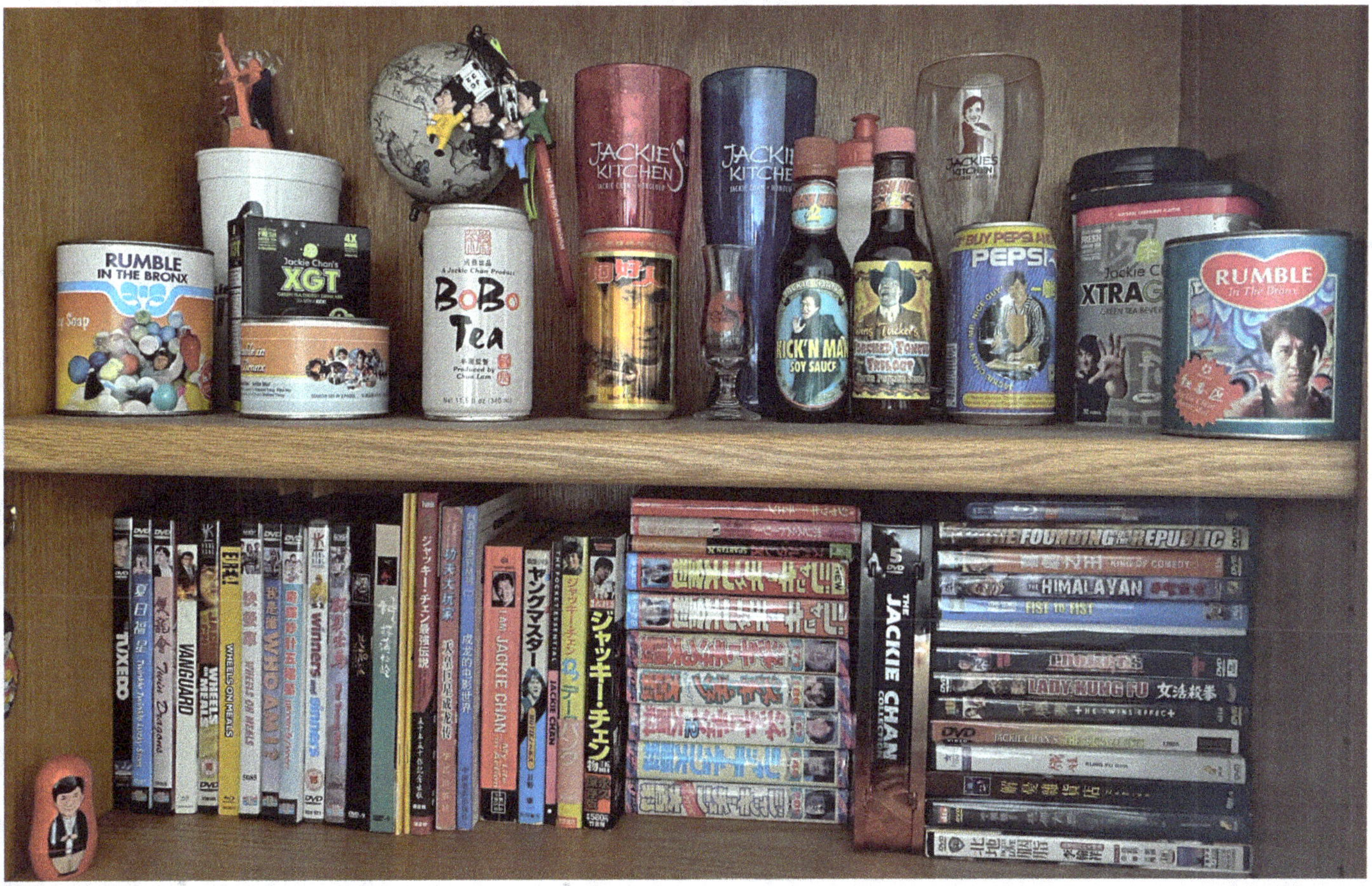
RUMBLE IN THE BRONX
Jackie Chan's XGT
BoBo Tea
JACKIE'S KITCHEN
KICK'N MAN SOY SAUCE
PEPSI
XTRA
RUMBLE In The Bronx
TUXEDO
VANGUARD
WHEELS ON MEALS
ヤングマスター
ジャッキー・チェン
JACKIE CHAN
THE JACKIE CHAN COLLECTION
THE FOUNDING OF A REPUBLIC
HIMALAYA N
FIST to FIST
LADY KUNG FU

- Magazines featuring him on the cover. This was the original "theme" for my collecting pursuits, I started with a few available magazines and ended up with over a thousand of them from every corner of the world, each one individually sealed and stored in binders across multiple shelves.

- Items signed by him, such as posters, photos, cards, books, magazines. Some of them personalized for me during our mutual encounters.

- Books about him from different countries and languages, such as his autobiography I Am Jackie Chan, his newer books, biographies by other authors, film guides, comic books, catalogs, photo albums, and other publications.

- DVDs, Blu-rays, VHS tapes, Laserdiscs of his films, both official and unofficial releases of all kinds. I have also collected some of his early works that are hard to find, interviews, fan-made compilations, concerts, commercials, behind-the-scenes, and more.

- CDs, vinyl LP and 45 records of his own discography, as well as soundtrack of his movies, DVDs and VHS tapes of his music videos, Karaoke versions and more.

- Posters, press kits, Japanese pamphlets and flyers, photo collections, 35mm slides, film strips, and more. Some of them are official, while others are unofficial or private.

- Action figures, resin statues, and promotional dolls of his characters or movies, some of them being limited editions or exclusives, while others are mass-produced to promote his films in different areas of the world.

- Clothing and accessories, such as T-shirts, jackets, hats, shoes, sunglasses, watches, keychains, umbrellas, etc. Some of them are official merchandise, while others are fan-made or customized.

- Other miscellaneous items related to him or his movies, such as stickers, stamps, pins, buttons, patches, magnets, mugs, plates, coasters, pens, rulers, notebooks, cards, videogames, and toys.

- Last but not least, I have a Jackie Chan vintage Pachinko machine, a mechanical game originating in Japan that is a mixture of slot machine and pinball, featuring lots of interesting videoclips of Jackie performing through the game.

After collecting for over 40 years, the story and thrill of obtaining some of these rare items is very valuable to me. They remind me of the joy and inspiration that Jackie's amazing career and achievements has brought to my life and millions of others around the world.

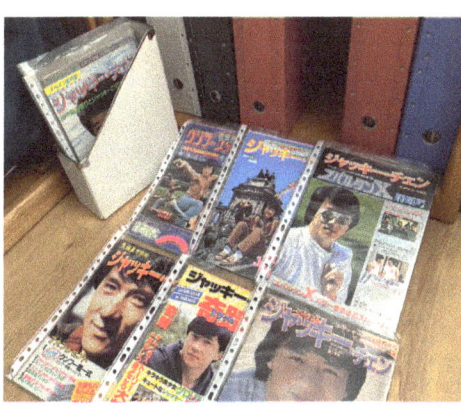

SELECTED POSTER GALLERY

羅維影業公司立體新貢獻
監製・導演 羅維
原著 古龍
攝影 陳榮樹
成龍・田俊・梁小龍 領銜主演
汪萍 領銜主演
鹿村 方芳 客串
出品人 許麗華
主題曲「飛渡捲雲山」
作曲：楊道火
作詞：麥青
主唱：巨人三重唱
盒帶由麗風唱片有限公司供應
Jacky Chan James Tien Leung Siu Lung
in
飛渡捲雲山
A LO WEI PRESENTATION
3D
MAGNIFICENT BODYGUARDS

ยิ่งใหญ่เหนือประวัติการณ์
มโหฬารเหนืออนาคต...
สุดยอดแห่งปี 22
เฉินหลง
ลบสถิติภาพยนตร์
ทำเองทุกเรื่อง
笑拳怪招
ซุปเปอร์มันส์!
ซุปเปอร์ฮา!
"THE FEARLESS HYENA"
สโคป•สี

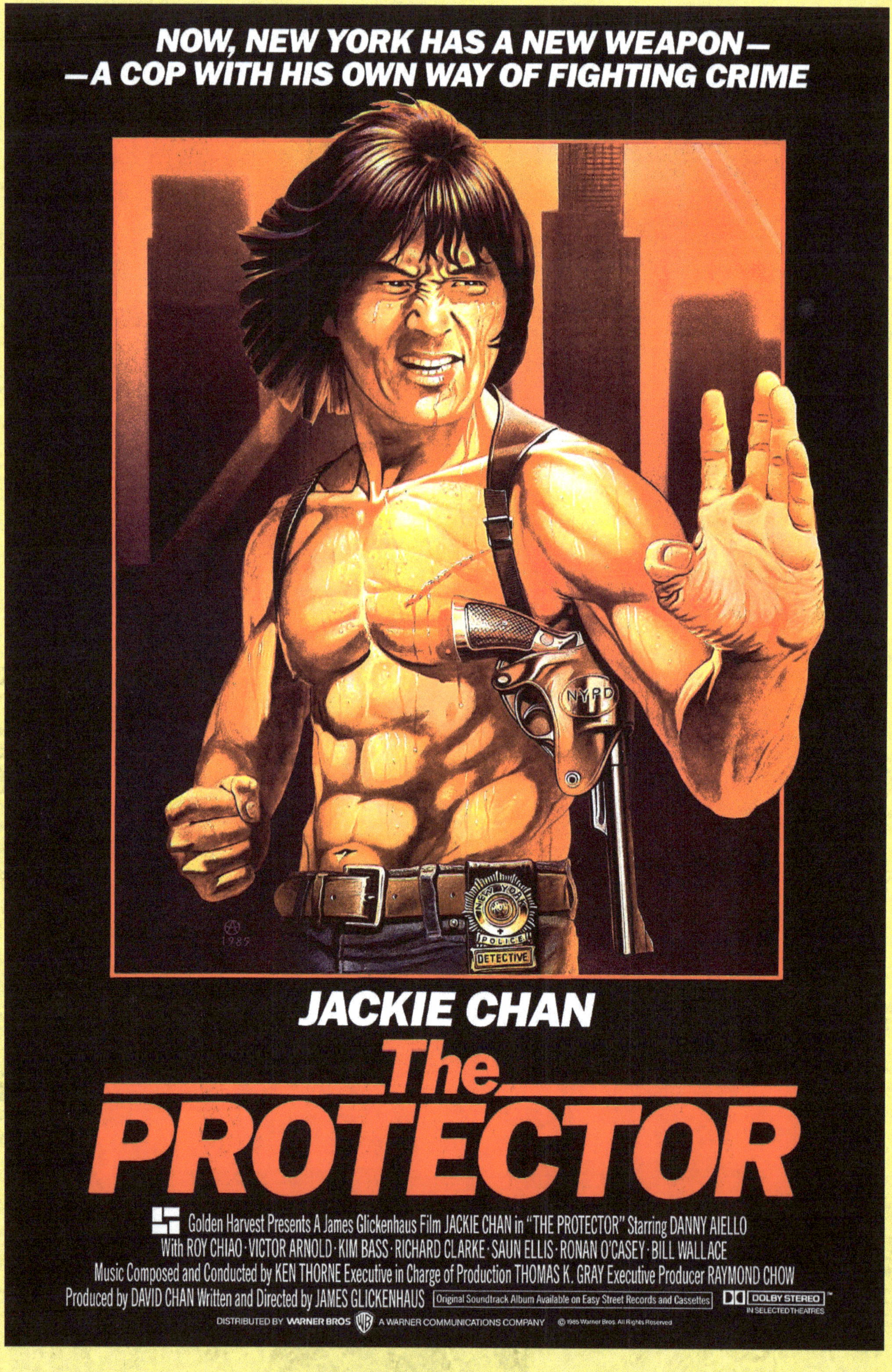
NOW, NEW YORK HAS A NEW WEAPON—
—A COP WITH HIS OWN WAY OF FIGHTING CRIME
NYPD
NEW YORK
POLICE
DETECTIVE
1985
JACKIE CHAN
The
PROTECTOR
Golden Harvest Presents A James Glickenhaus Film JACKIE CHAN in "THE PROTECTOR" Starring DANNY AIELLO
With ROY CHIAO · VICTOR ARNOLD · KIM BASS · RICHARD CLARKE · SAUN ELLIS · RONAN O'CASEY · BILL WALLACE
Music Composed and Conducted by KEN THORNE Executive in Charge of Production THOMAS K. GRAY Executive Producer RAYMOND CHOW
Produced by DAVID CHAN Written and Directed by JAMES GLICKENHAUS
Original Soundtrack Album Available on Easy Street Records and Cassettes
DOLBY STEREO
IN SELECTED THEATRES
DISTRIBUTED BY WARNER BROS A WARNER COMMUNICATIONS COMPANY
© 1985 Warner Bros. All Rights Reserved

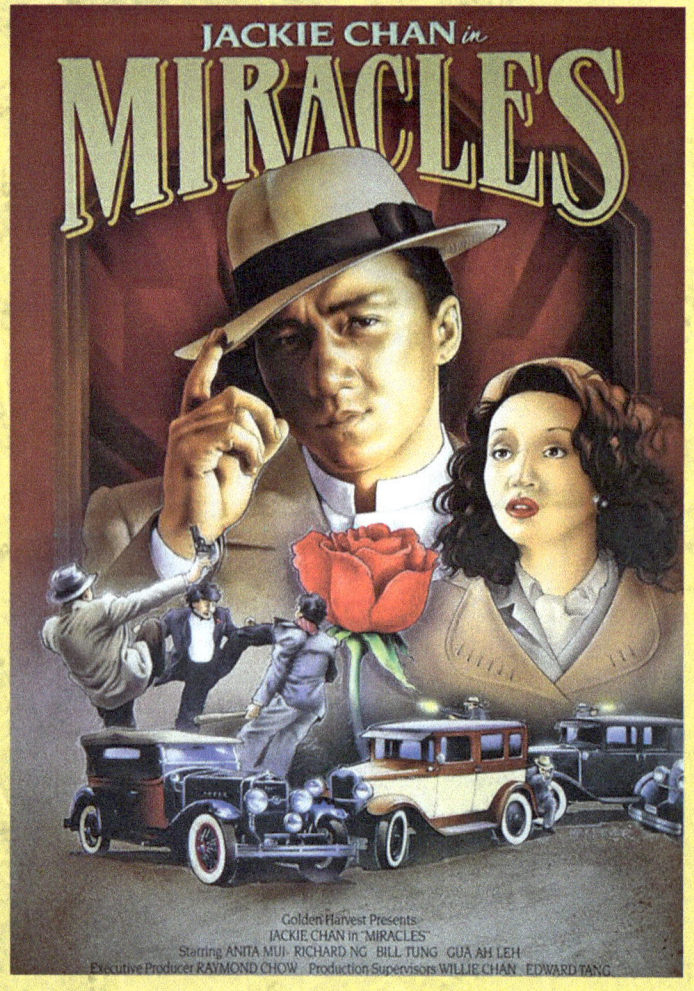

CITY HUNTER
城市獵人
CITY HUNTER

重案組

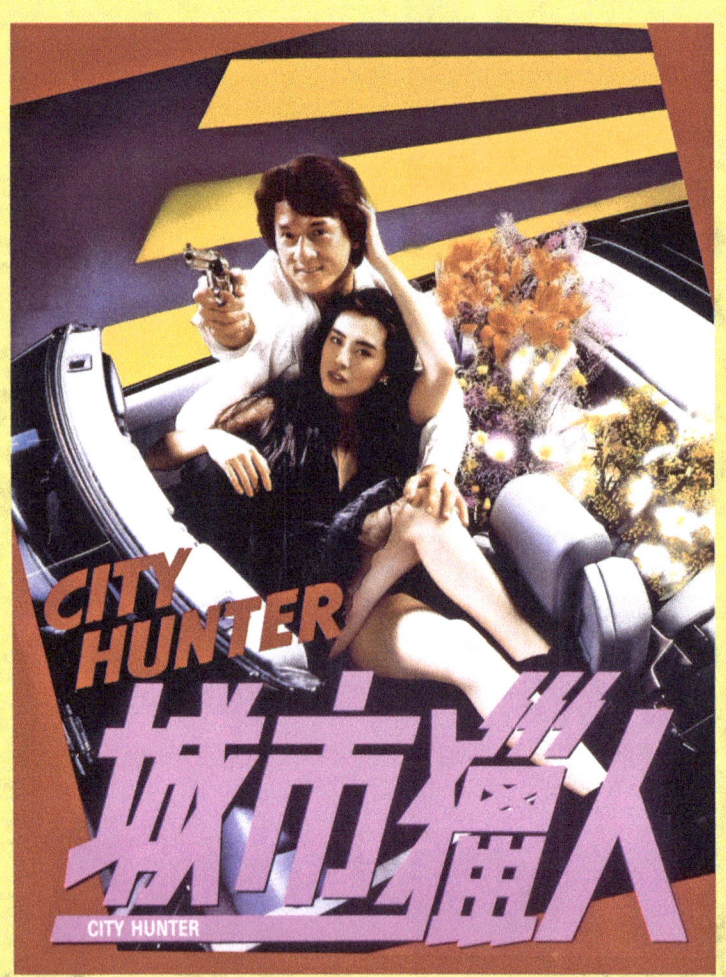

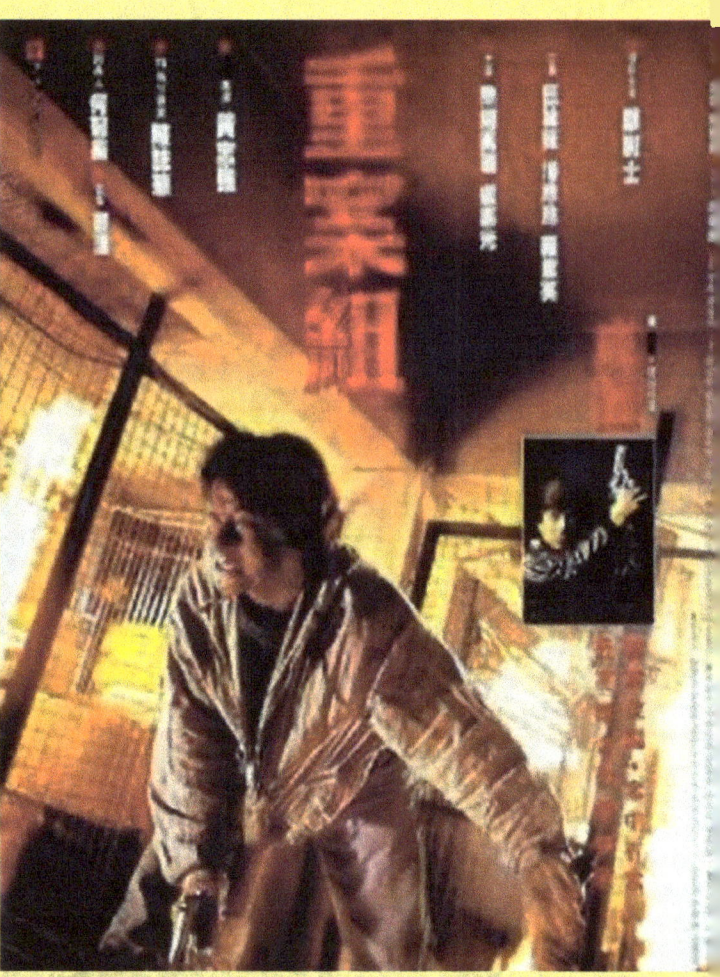

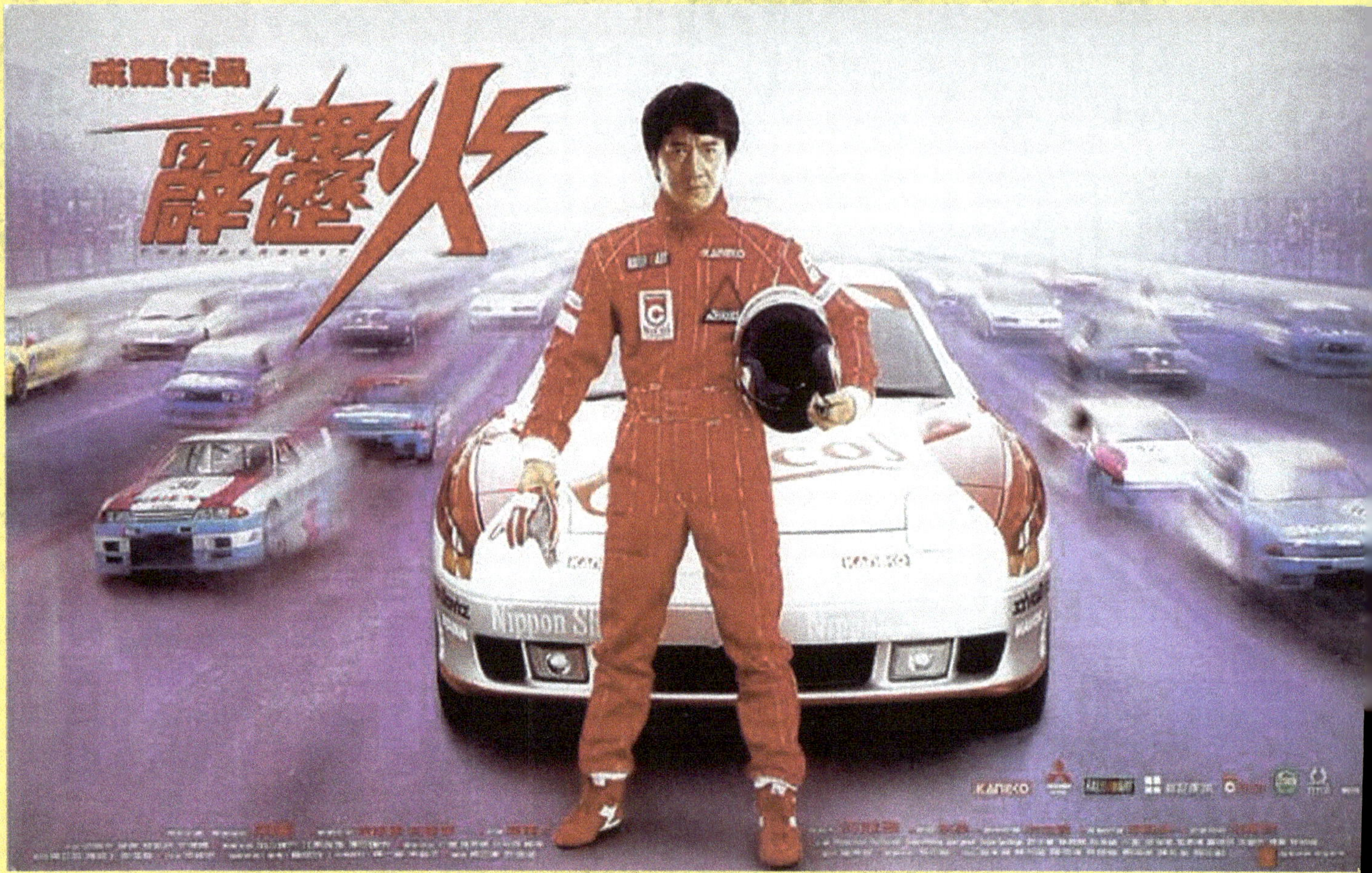
成龍作品
霹靂火

www.ingramcontent.com/pod-product-compliance
Lightning Source LLC
Chambersburg PA
CBHW061151010526
44118CB00026B/2940